Friends

Pursuing and Developing Godly Friendships

NANCY AVERA

long with the Women's Ministry Team at NorthPointe Community Church

FRIENDS
Pursuing and Developing Godly Friendships

ISBN: 978-0-9915559-9-4
Published by PMT Publishing, Fresno, California

EDITORIAL TEAM

Content Editor
Rhonda Blackburn

Assistant Content Editor
Ashlie Graef

NorthPointe Women's Ministry Team
Kasey Jackson
Christy Manning
Cindy Patzkowsky

DEDICATION

For all who desire deep and meaningful friendships.

May you always be blessed with Godly friends.

Nancy Avera

TABLE OF CONTENTS

WHY YOU NEED GODLY FRIENDS

PROFILE OF A GODLY FRIEND

UNHEALTHY FRIENDSHIPS

WALKING IN DAY TO DAY FRIENDSHIP

APPENDICES

INTRODUCTION

We live in a world where deep and meaningful friendships are hard to find. Often we're suspicious of others and insecure about ourselves. So, we withdraw to the safety of our self-made digital worlds.

But sister, you were made for community. Yes, you. God designed you this way. Since this is part of your design, the enemy of God (Satan) wants you to isolate. He will fill your head with lies to keep you from connecting with godly people, especially in times of difficulties.

Making friends comes more naturally for some people than others. Your personality type, disposition, and life experiences impact how you feel about the subject of this Bible study. But one thing is certain, the Bible has a lot to say about what makes a good friend.

The purpose of this Bible study is two-fold:
- To help you grow in your faith and understanding of God and His Word.

- To challenge and encourage you to be a godly friend and pursue deep friendships.

If you're anything like me, you have had times in your life when you truly needed a friend; but instead of reaching out, you yielded to thoughts like these:
- I don't want to bother anyone with my problems.

- Compared to other people, what I'm going through is no big deal.

- I don't feel like being around people right now; I would rather be alone.

- Nobody notices when I'm not at church, so why bother?

You and I need community. So let's commit to pursuing God's Word together over the next four weeks and ask Him to help us develop rich friendships. Real friendships can be costly. Love does make us vulnerable. But without risk, we will never experience the fullness of Christ.

1

Godly friendship exists <u>because</u> of Christ and <u>for</u> Christ.

WHY YOU NEED GODLY FRIENDS

Introduction

Before you jump into each assignment, ask God to be with you, to help you focus on His Word, and teach you what He wants you to know today. Check out the sample prayer below if you need help, or pray what naturally comes to mind. Be honest with God about how you feel going into this Bible Study. Some of us are entering in because we don't have close friends and we really want that in our lives. If that's you, take heart, you are not alone. Others may be entering in because of the fellowship, but feel there's nothing new to learn about this topic. If that's you, then I encourage you to be open – God might have some surprises in store!

LET'S PRAY

Jesus, I worship you in spirit and truth and ask that you would lead me and guide me as I open your Word. You said in John 15:17, "This is my command: Love each other." I confess that I need your help to love others the way you love me. Please teach me about myself and what I need to learn to be a better friend. In Jesus' name, Amen.

In Jonathan Holmes' book, *The Company We Keep: In Search of Biblical Friendship* he defines biblical friendship this way:

"Biblical friendship exists when two or more people, bound together by a common faith in Jesus Christ, pursue him and his kingdom with intentionality and vulnerability. Rather than serving as an end in itself, biblical friendship serves primarily to bring glory to Christ, who brought us into friendship with the Father. It is indispensable to the work of the gospel in the earth, and an essential element of what God created us for."

Here's what we'll be looking at in Week 1.

- **Day 1** – You Need Friends because God Designed You for Community.
- **Day 2** – You Need Friends for Spiritual Growth.
- **Day 3** – You Need Friends for Encouragement/Emotional Support.
- **Day 4** – You Need Friends to Celebrate Wins.
- **Day 5** – You Need Friends to Share in the Losses of Life.

Biblical friendship serves primarily to bring glory to Christ.

DAY 1 – YOU NEED FRIENDS BECAUSE GOD DESIGNED YOU FOR COMMUNITY

1. Describe a time when a friend was a true help to you. Or, how has God been a true friend to you?

   _____

   _____

   _____

   _____

   _____

GOD DESIGNED US FOR FRIENDSHIP

2. Read the passage below and mark the plural pronouns in the passage (e.g., we, us).

   "Then God said, "Let Us make mankind in Our image, in Our likeness, so that they may rule over the fish in the sea and the birds in the sky, over the livestock and all the wild animals, and over all the creatures that move along the ground. So God created mankind in His own image, in the image of God He created them." Genesis 1:26-27

3. What does it say about how you were created?

   _____

   _____

> " A sweet friendship refreshes the soul.
> —————— Proverbs 27:9

4. Look up and read Genesis 2:18. What is not good?

_____

5. How do these two passages (Genesis 1:26-27 and 2:18) impact your understanding of community?

_____
_____
_____

From the very beginning, the Bible tells us that we were created to enjoy a relationship with God (Genesis 1).

In an article entitled, "10 Biblical Truths about Real Friendship," author Drew Hunter states,

"At each step of the way when God created the world, he pronounced that everything was "good." But then once he created Adam, a statement startles us: something is not good. "It is not good that the man should be alone" (Genesis 2:18). This was before the fall — before sin had entered the world. Solitude came before sin.

From the very beginning, the Bible tells us that we were created to enjoy a relationship with God (Genesis 1). God exists in community as the Father, Son, and the Holy Spirit. We were made in His image. We also learn that we were created for relationships with each other (Genesis 2). The creation of Eve isn't just the story of marriage, it's also the beginning of community.

It can be hard for some of us to commit to community, especially if we're shy, we've been hurt, or we simply prefer solitude. It can drain our energy, be uncomfortable at times, or even require a sacrifice on our part. But community is God's desire for us, and a sign of a mature faith.

6. Is there anything inside of you that resists this truth? Can you identify what thoughts or fears you are pushing back?

_____
_____
_____
_____
_____
_____
_____

The Bible says the Holy Spirit is present whenever believers gather together. A great example of this is the early church of Acts that made a habit of meeting together, eating together, and worshiping together. As a result, "the Lord added to their number daily those who were being saved" (Acts 2:46–47).

God exists in community as the Father, Son, and the Holy Spirit.

7. According to the following passages, why should you choose to engage in community?

- Matthew 18:20 _____

- Romans 12:4-6 _____

- Psalm 133:1 _____

_____

KEY POINTS

- God exists within community.

- He created us in His image.

- It is not good to be alone.

- Sometimes we avoid community when we should pursue it.

- The Holy Spirit reveals His presence to us directly and also through those gathered around us, in His name.

Friendship Challenge #1

Close your time by praying and asking God to ...

1. Open your heart to the idea of deep friendships and living in community.

2. Bless your current friends.

3. Reveal where you need to step out in faith to be a better friend.

DAY 2 — YOU NEED FRIENDS FOR SPIRITUAL GROWTH

You don't need a lot of friends — you just need a few really good ones. Meaningful friends help you achieve what you would never have been able to without them. But sister, if you think your life is too busy and you don't have the time to foster deep friendships, you need good friends more than you realize. Since we are created in the image of God, you will see aspects of Christ in others that you can't grasp if you're staying detached from fellow image-bearers. You can't be like Christ and isolate yourself from others.

1. Think about a friend who has helped you grow spiritually. What has the person done to encourage you in your faith? If you can't think of a friend, ask yourself, "How have I encouraged a friend to grow spiritually?"

   _____

   _____

   _____

   _____

   _____

FIRST THINGS FIRST

In John 15:12-17, Jesus is talking with his disciples. As you read this verse, mark the commands.

"This is My commandment, that you love one another as I have loved you. Greater love has no one than this, that he lay down his life for his friends. You are My friends if you do what I command you. No longer do I call you servants, for a servant does not understand what his master is doing. But I have called you friends, because everything I have learned from My Father I have made known to you. You did not choose Me, but I chose you. And I appointed you to go and bear fruit — fruit that will remain — so that whatever you ask the Father in My name, He will give you. This is My command to you: Love one another."

It is not possible for us to love each other without the love of Christ in us. Would you seriously lay down your life for your friend? It's a nice thought and a familiar Bible verse, but frankly, we're just too stinkin' selfish to lay our lives down. Heck, sometimes we don't even want to rearrange our schedule to meet with a friend!

We must look to Christ as the example of friendship. If our friendships are going to bear fruit, we must encourage and challenge each other in our faith journey, always pointing our friends to Christ.

Godly friends are willing to speak the truth with love and grace, even when it is uncomfortable.

BRINGING OUT THE BEST IN YOU

2. Read Romans 1:11-12. Why did Paul want to see his friends in Rome?

_____

_____

_____

3. Read Hebrews 10:24–25. What does this passage tell you to do?

_____

_____

4. Look again at Hebrews 10:24–25. What does this passage tell you NOT to do?

_____

We strengthen each other when we're together. There's something unique about being with a girlfriend. Whether it's a walk through the park, a cup of coffee, or a long-distance FaceTime call, we must not give up meeting together to encourage each other.

WISDOM AND ACTION

The book of Proverbs has a lot to say about friendship. The primary purpose is to teach wisdom and provide insights on how to live a happy and peaceful life by honoring and respecting God as all-good and all-powerful. Let's look at a few Proverbs.

5. Read and write Proverbs 27:5-6

    _____

    _____

    _____

6. Read and write Proverbs 27:17

    _____

    _____

We also learn in Proverbs 24 that,

"An honest answer is a sign of a true friendship." Proverbs 24:26 TEV

Godly friends are willing to speak the truth with love and grace, even when it's uncomfortable. It's so much easier for us to be loving and encouraging than it is to say the hard stuff like, "You might be angry at me for saying this, but I care more about your future and our friendship than I do my feelings of rejection. I think what you're about to do is a mistake."

7. Do you have anyone in your life that you've given permission to speak up when they think you're wrong? Would you be willing to bravely ask God for this type of friendship? Write a prayer asking God to bring someone into your life that can be this kind of friend. If you do have a such a friend, write a prayer of thanks.

    _____

    _____

    _____

    _____

    _____

    _____

    _____

Friendship Challenge
#2

**Take action from
Hebrews 10:24-25
by reaching out to a friend
and asking her to meet.**

DAY 3 – YOU NEED FRIENDS FOR ENCOURAGEMENT/ EMOTIONAL SUPPORT

Anne throws up a post on Facebook that says, "I don't know how I'm going to get through this day."

You see Suzy in Sunday service with tears running down her face.

Sara snaps at you for something trivial, and you realize there's a deeper pain causing her reaction.

We have all seen people struggling with life to varying degrees. Sometimes we know the cause of their pain – they've had a loss of some kind. But often we know there's "something" but it is an unknown. I'm reasonably certain, too, that we all have second guessed ourselves wondering how to respond, or IF to respond. Should I invite myself into their experience, or should I wait for an invitation? Is my genuine concern going to feel pushy instead of loving? What if I say/do the wrong thing?

The same is true when we're the ones struggling and need to reach out for support. Sometimes it's difficult to understand how to ask for help. Frankly, sometimes we're both wishing someone will notice us, and at the same time scared to death that they will.

Life is messy.

We all need loving, emotional support – sometimes more than others. But God doesn't specify to only encourage someone when it seems needed; rather, He just says to do it! Frankly, we don't always know when it is needed, but God does.

When you have a friend who's going through a tough season, how do you respond? A quick text? Maybe a phone call? A prayer? An invitation for coffee? Perhaps you back off to give her space to work things out on her own. There's a risk while engaging with someone in need, and we must have healthy boundaries that we'll talk about in a future lesson. But for now, let's see what God's Word has to say about offering encouragement to our friends.

1. What do you typically do when you're discouraged? List positive and negative things. Be honest.

   _____

   _____

   _____

2. Look up and write Galatians 6:2.

   _____

   _____

3. What are we instructed to do in 1 Thessalonians 5:11?

   _____

   _____

> " God knows that we need each other and that we need Him at the center of our friendships.

Check out this passage from Ecclesiastes 4:9-12 and jot down what stands out to you from the verses.

"Two are better than one, because they have a good reward for their toil. For if they fall, one will lift up his fellow. But woe to him who is alone when he falls and has not another to lift him up! Again, if two lie together, they keep warm, but how can one keep warm alone? And though a man might prevail against one who is alone, two will withstand him—a threefold cord is not quickly broken."

_____

_____

_____

_____

You + your friend + God = a threefold cord. Can I get an Amen?

ONE ANOTHERS

The phrase "one another" is derived from the Greek word "allelon," which means "one another, each other; mutually, reciprocally." It occurs almost 60 times in the New Testament and teaches us how (and how not) to relate to one another.

Spiritual growth requires that we follow God's commands on how to treat one another. It is a great way to guide our friendships. Jesus said,

"A new command I give you: Love one another. As I have loved you, so you must love one another. By this everyone will know that you are my disciples, if you love one another." John 13:34-35

By the way, this command, "love one another," occurs at least 16 times in the New Testament.

Obedience to these commands is essential. It forms the basis for all real Christian community and directly impacts our ability to show the world that Christian friendship is different. Loving one another is both attitude and action. It's not merely stating "I love you" because I'm a Christian, and I'm supposed to. It's allowing people to see the love of God in our everyday interactions with our friends.

LOOK UP THE FOLLOWING "ONE ANOTHER" SCRIPTURES AND WRITE THE COMMAND

Don't worry, they're not long and they're in order. 😊

1. Romans 12:10

_____

2. Romans 12:16

_____

3. Romans 15:7

_____

4. 1 Corinthians 12:25

_____

5. Galatians 6:2

_____

6. Ephesians 4:32

_____

7. Colossians 3:16

_____

8. 1 Thessalonians 4:18

_____

DO'S AND DON'TS OF EMOTIONAL SUPPORT

- **DO** reach out to connect and listen.

- **DO** practice being present without words.

- **DO** acknowledge her pain.

- **DO** speak words that build her up.

- **DO** ask questions – "How are you feeling today?" "What can I do to help?" "How can I pray for you?"

- **DO** keep the focus on her.

We need to lift each other up, learn from one another, and be the friend each of us needs.

- **DON'T** try to solve her problems.

- **DON'T** minimize her struggle.

- **DON'T** preach a sermon.

- **DON'T** make it about you.

- **DON'T** forget to follow up.

- **DON'T** be afraid of silence.

9. What else would you add to this list?

_____

_____

_____

_____

_____

Learning to support our friends emotionally takes practice, but it does get easier the more often you sit with hurting people. I love the way the Amplified paraphrase of the Bible renders this familiar verse out of James. Check it out:

"Understand this, my beloved brothers and sisters. Let everyone be quick to hear [be a careful, thoughtful listener], slow to speak [a speaker of carefully chosen words and], slow to anger [patient, reflective, forgiving];" James 1:19

Friendship Challenge
#3

Pick 2 or 3 passages from the
"One Another Section"
and put them into practice
this week!

DAY 4 — YOU NEED FRIENDS TO CELEBRATE WINS

1. What's the first thing you do when you get good news?

   _____

   _____

   _____

2. If you answered, "I thank God," then what's the next thing you do?

   _____

   _____

Enjoyment and celebration are fantastic (albeit obvious) reasons you need friends. When I get good news, I can't wait to tell someone I love. Sharing personal victories, promotions at work, or expanding families are just a few life experiences that need to be celebrated. And, let's be honest, sharing victories on social media is not the same thing as sharing face-to-face with a friend.

3. Read Proverbs 17:22 and write in your own words.

   _____

   _____

   _____

I love the way the New Living Translation renders this verse, check it out:

"A cheerful heart is good medicine, but a broken spirit saps a person's strength." Proverbs 17:22

You've experienced both sides of this equation, haven't you? When you have deep and meaningful friendships, you have people that will be with you when your heart is cheerful AND when your spirit is crushed.

SCIENCE UNCOVERED WHAT GOD ALREADY LAID OUT

It always makes me smile when science supports something that God's Word declared to be right thousands of years ago. In Psalm 144:15 we read,

"Happy are the people whose God is the LORD."

We know that God is the true source of happiness, strength, hope, and wisdom. But sometimes the world needs "evidence of things unseen."

Check out what this article reported in "CNN Health" that links happiness with life expectancy.

- The five-year study of people age 52 to 79 discovered that the people who reported feeling happy, excited, and content on a typical day were 35% less likely to die.

- Regions of the brain involved in happiness are also engaged in blood-vessel function and inflammation.

- Studies have shown that levels of the stress hormone Cortisol tend to rise and fall with emotion.

It is good for your body and your soul to be happy.

1. Read Nehemiah 8:10. What does the Lord instruct his people to do after they heard His Word?

_____

Our response as followers of Christ should be the same. Rejoice. Together. The Bible is full of stories about praising God for all the great things He does for us, and it's so much sweeter when we rejoice within the context of community. Yes, It's OK for Christians to party! In a healthy way, of course!

"Rejoice in the Lord always: and again I say, Rejoice."

Philippians 4:4

> ❝ All throughout the Bible we observe early Christians living, enjoying, and celebrating life together.

LET US REJOICE

In the story of The Prodigal Son (Luke 15:11-32), we see a father embrace a wayward son and throw a party when he returns home.

When Mary, the mother of Jesus, visits with her cousin Elizabeth in the first chapter of Luke, we observe the sweet relationship between these women who embrace, praise God, and sing.

As Paul and Barnabas share the Good News, and the Word of the Lord was spreading throughout the whole region, we see their joy in Scripture.

"And the disciples were filled with joy and with the Holy Spirit" Acts 13:52 ESV

5. Read Acts 2:46-47 and write what the early Christians did together.

   _____

   _____

MORE JOY SCRIPTURES

- *"Rejoice with those who rejoice; mourn with those who mourn." Romans 12:15a*

- *"Let them praise his name with dancing, making melody to him with tambourine and lyre!" Psalm 149:3*

- *"Let us come before His presence with thanksgiving. Let us shout joyfully to Him with psalms." Psalm 95:2*

- *"From them will proceed thanksgiving and the voice of those who celebrate; And I will multiply them and they will not be diminished; I will also honor them and they will not be insignificant." Jeremiah 30:19*

GIRLS JUST WANNA HAVE FUN

When we pursue Christ-like friendships, we have the freedom to respond with all kinds of fun, but be careful as you express your joy to heed the warnings of Proverbs 13:20.

6. Read Proverbs 13:20 and write in your own words

_____

_____

_____

In the first verse of Romans Chapter 6, we read about the principle of being dead to sin and alive in Christ.

"What shall we say, then? Shall we go on sinning so that grace may increase? By no means! We are those who have died to sin; how can we live in it any longer?" Romans 6:1

You get the point. Don't be rejoicing by getting drunk, loud, and obnoxious in the name of Jesus.

7. Think about your personal life, does having fun with your friends reflect God? Why or why not?

_____

_____

_____

_____

Friendship Challenge #4

Is there anything you need to change when having fun with your friends to better honor God?

DAY 5 – YOU NEED FRIENDS TO SHARE IN THE LOSSES OF LIFE

1. Think of a time of loss in your life. Maybe it was the passing of a loved one, the loss of a job, a divorce, the death of a dream, or your health. Was there someone who shared this time with you? What made you feel seen during that time?

    _____

    _____

    _____

    _____

We are called to be good friends during good times and bad. In fact, it is during hardships that our friendships deepen. Sometimes just being present with someone is the most powerful act you can do as a friend.

In talking about the unity and diversity in the body of Christ, Paul, in his first letter to the Corinthian church, compares a human body to the body of Christ. He talks about how different parts have different jobs and that we all need to work together.

2. Read 1 Corinthians 12:26 and write it in your own words.

    _____

    _____

    _____

3. Read 2 Corinthians 1:3-4. In this passage, we are assured that God will comfort us. What else do you notice about the message of these verses?

_____

_____

_____

We know from reading the New Testament that Jesus wept when his good friend died (John 11:35).

In Job Chapter 2 we see Job's friends weep and enter into his sorrow. They sat with him for seven days and nights without saying a word because they "saw how intense his suffering had become" (Job 2:12-13). These dear friends gave Job the gift of their presence. No words were needed.

When we're in pain, it can cause us to doubt our faith or question God. And that's OK!

ENTERING IN

In Galatians we find one of the most important ways that believers can serve one another. We are told that we must "bear one another's burdens," and that by doing so we will fulfill the law of Christ. As Christians, we fulfill the law of Jesus the Messiah by being present with people.

4. Read Galatians 6:2 and write in your own words.

_____

_____

_____

_____

5. Read 1 Corinthians 2:3 and write in your own words.

_____

_____

_____

LEARNING TO LISTEN

6. What is the message of James 1:19?

_____

_____

_____

- Listen to the emotions AND the words.

- Listen without interruption.

- Listen for what they aren't saying.

- Ask yourself, how would I feel if this were happening to me?

- Sit a while. Don't try to fix. Just be there.

ACCEPT DOUBT AND QUESTIONS

When we're in pain, it can cause us to doubt our faith or question God. That doesn't happen to everyone, but it's alright if it happens to you. It's reasonable to ask God hard questions and express your real emotions to the Lord. He can handle it, and it's a healthy part of the healing.

7. Reflect on a time when you were in a season of pain, doubt, anger, or just distant from God. What kinds of questions and doubts did you have at that time?

_____

_____

_____

_____

_____

_____

Friendship Challenge
#5

Ask the Lord to reveal to you someone in your life that is hurting and how you could lovingly respond.

2

Our friendships should foster dependence on God, not just on one another.

PROFILE OF A GODLY FRIEND

Introduction

Biblical friendship is when two or more people, bound together through the power of the Holy Spirit, pursue Christ, His kingdom, and healthy relationships with intentionality and vulnerability.

Biblical friendship serves primarily to bring glory to Christ, who brought us into friendship with the Father. So, biblical friendship must begin with our friendship with Christ.

Biblical friendship must be centered on Christ and bound together by His sacrificial death on the cross. A bond built on anything less will never have the same satisfaction, survive the tests, or bear the same fruit. The Bible tells us that through Christ we are actually in a friendship relationship with Christ Himself (John 15:15). If that doesn't stop you in your tracks, I don't know what will! The concept of friendship is indeed a spiritual one; and as followers of Christ, we all have at least one friend in common (Jesus) who sets the example for us to follow – if we're willing.

IT'S COMPLICATED

Cultivating deep friendships can be messy, and many barriers can keep us from wanting to develop close and intimate relationships.

Lack of trust. Past hurt. Fear of being known and not loved. Society's pressures to maintain an image – an image that might burst if someone knew the truth.

These things can keep us from pursuing a more meaningful relationship with friends. After all, we might think, "If I open myself up to you, then you'll see me for who I really am. What if you reject that ... reject ME?" When you get close, there is a risk of hurt, and most of us would rather avoid hurt or conflict. Our list of excuses can be long, but when we focus on developing godly relationships we'll soon discover that the list of benefits makes it worth the risk.

Yes, the pursuit of meaningful relationship requires a certain amount of boldness! But I'll say it again: The benefits and rewards of a trusted friendship far outweigh the awkward and uncomfortable moments that can be created when we are transparent, humble, empathetic, and intentional.

In this week's study, we are going to define characteristics of godly friendships. We will:

- Consider how God uses deep friendships to help us become more like Him.

- Learn that we are not alone in our insecurities, fears, dreams, and values.

- Discover times when we have been able to borrow someone's faith and learn from their experiences.

- Explore a biblical gauge by which we can measure ourselves when reflecting on the kind of friend we want and need to be.

LET'S PRAY

Jesus, thank you for your faithfulness and goodness in our lives. We ask you to open the eyes of our hearts as we study your Word. Thank you for the gift of companionship in our friendships. There is no more significant friend than you, Lord, for you are love. Be with us now as we draw into your presence. In Jesus' name, Amen.

DAY 1 — A GODLY FRIEND IS HUMBLE

1. When you think of the word "humility," what positive and negative thoughts come to mind?

   _____

   _____

   _____

"Humility is not thinking less of yourself; it's thinking of yourself less."

CS Lewis

In our society, especially in the workplace, an attitude of "my way or the highway" can be dominant. It can pop up in marriages and in the church, too! But in Paul's letter to the Philippians, he writes about Christ's way and the importance of imitating Christ's life of humility.

The Christian motivation for humility is rooted in submission to God. When we recognize how truly all powerful, magnificent, and glorious God is, it is easy to humble ourselves before Him. As we gain a more accurate view of who we are and who HE is, it can be wonderfully overwhelming to come to grips with how much He loves and cares for us.

Look up and read Philippians 2:1-5 about imitating Christ's humility, then fill in your answers below.

2. Make a list of all the things Paul says we share because we are united with Christ (verses 1 and 2). Here's a partial list to get you started: encouragement, comfort, sharing in the spirit,

   _____

   _____

   _____

3. What do verses 3 & 4 instruct us NOT to do?

   _____

4. What do verses 3 & 4 tell us we should do as followers of Jesus?

   _____

   _____

5. In what ways do you find yourself struggling with selfishness or conceit in friendships?

_____

_____

_____

_____

_____

_____

SORRY VERSUS I WAS WRONG

When my husband and I were young parents, we received some profound advice that we implemented with our boys and instilled in our marriage. When reconciling after any conflict, we choose to first and foremost acknowledge the wrongdoing. We encouraged our kids to say, "I'm sorry," and prayed that they would be repentant, but we didn't require it.

Let me give you an example. When four-year-old Ben threw a book at his two-year-old brother, Will, we could have required him to say, "I'm sorry," which is appropriate and biblical. But the problem is that repentance is a heart issue. Picture an irritated four-year-old, arms crossed, jaw clenched, squeaking out the words, "soorrrryyy" just to move on with the day. Not so meaningful, right?

Now let's flip the script in the same situation.

The book is still flung through the air at the younger brother. There is still screaming and parental intervention. This time the resolution looks like this: "Will, I was wrong for throwing the book at you. I was wrong for losing my temper. Will you please forgive me?"

You can feel the difference, can't you?

We cannot force anyone to be sorry, but we can learn to acknowledge the truth of our sin. This is a practice that takes humility. We discovered that with practice it got easier for our boys (and for us) to acknowledge the sin of being wrong. Later, true repentance came in the form of an apology, too.

6. Do you find it hard to admit to yourself and/or others when you're wrong? Explain.

_____

_____

_____

_____

The Hebrew word most often translated "exalt," is rum and it means to lift up, or to become higher.

THE UPSIDE-DOWN KINGDOM

Throughout the New Testament, Jesus describes and demonstrates the importance of taking the posture of humility. For example, The Parable of the Wedding Feast (Luke 14:7-11) ends with this verse,

> *"For everyone who exalts himself will be humbled, and he who humbles himself will be exalted."*

In James 4:10 we read,

> *"Humble yourselves before the Lord, and he will exalt you."*

7. Another example is found in Colossians 3:12-14 below. As you read the passage, circle the characteristics we are to put on each day.

> *"Therefore, as God's chosen people, holy and dearly loved, clothe yourselves with compassion, kindness, humility, gentleness and patience. Bear with each other and forgive one another if any of you has a grievance against someone. Forgive as the Lord forgave you. And over all these virtues put on love, which binds them all together in perfect unity."*

A HEART OF SERVICE

Christian friends are not selfish. They do not use their friends to meet their needs, but humbly and sacrificially serve those whom Christ has called them to love. He gave us the vivid example of this when He stooped down to wash His disciples' feet.

"If I then, your Lord and Teacher, have washed your feet, you also ought to wash one another's feet. For I have given you an example, that you should do just as I have done to you." John 13:14-15 ESV

8. Considering the passages of Scripture you've read today, how can you show humility in your friendships this week? Be specific.

_____

_____

_____

_____

_____

9. What might make this challenging?

_____

_____

_____

_____

_____

Friendship Challenge #6

Look for ways to show humility in your friendships this week.

DAY 2 — A GODLY FRIEND IS TRANSPARENT & AUTHENTIC

1. What are your barriers to having deep relationships?

   _____

   _____

   _____

   _____

2. What do you think is the benefit of going deep?

   _____

   _____

   _____

   _____

"You will become way less concerned with what other people think of you when you realize how seldom they do."
– David Foster Wallace

Deep friendship is characterized by authenticity and transparency, which takes time. The purpose of transparency is to know each other better and to build each other up in Christ (1 Thessalonians 5:11).

Meaningful friendships require time, risk, and authenticity.

IT TAKES TIME

To know someone deeply, you need shared experiences. It is through the hills and valleys of everyday life that you learn someone's values, struggles, goals, and interests. Gratefully, the power of the Holy Spirit connects us with the common interests of God and many of the same core values.

May I encourage you to keep attending your small group and Bible studies? Keep investing your time by showing up. More often than not, you'll be glad you did. Remember, it is part of your discipleship to invest your time in the ways God tells you to. If you're "too busy" to connect with others, then I humbly suggest you are putting things into your life that God hasn't told you to. Some evaluation of how you invest your time may be required to root out the things God doesn't want there.

In Proverbs 18:24 we read,

> *"One who has unreliable friends soon comes to ruin, but there is a friend who sticks closer than a brother."*

Christ-like friends take time to form and even more time to develop. You need to nurture new connections, and you can do this by being interested and invested in other people.

3. Read Philippians 2:4 and record your thoughts.

_____

_____

_____

_____

We all have acquaintances, people we exchange small talk with as we go about our day. We have co-workers, childhood friends with decades of history, and people we've met at church or in our neighborhoods. While all of these relationships can be fulfilling in their own right, each of us long for deeper connections.

As relationships begin to deepen, you can ask yourself some questions to evaluate them after spending time together.

- Do I feel better after spending time with this person?

- Am I myself around this person?

- Do I feel secure, or do I feel like I have to watch what I say and do?

- Is the person supportive, and am I treated with respect?

- Is this a person I can trust?

RISKY BUSINESS

Friendships are more like dating than we admit. The principles are the same. A one-sided friendship is not a true friendship and is not what most people want! Moving from an acquaintance to a friend requires that you open up to the other person, and give them the freedom to open up to you. It's risky business, and too many of us let our insecurities get in the way of transparency and authenticity. Can you relate?

Mark the reasons below that might keep you from taking the risk of being transparent in a small group or one-on-one setting.

- ❑ My opinions, experiences, and feelings are not as important or interesting as other peoples'.
- ❑ I'm afraid of what people will think.
- ❑ I don't trust people/I've been hurt before.
- ❑ People won't agree with me or value my input.
- ❑ I'm worried I'll sound stupid.
- ❑ I'm afraid I'll be judged for my thoughts/feelings.
- ❑ If they really knew me, they wouldn't like me.
- ❑ I don't like people/I'm not a "people person."
- ❑ I'm an introvert, I prefer to be alone.
- ❑ I wonder if the other person even wants to be my friend; I fear rejection.
- ❑ I'm shy, I have a fear of talking or that I might talk too much.

AUTHENTICITY

Deep friendships can get messy, and there will be times that they are uncomfortable and hard. But if you're willing to take the risk – push through by being transparent and authentic – the fruit of your friendship will develop stronger roots in Christ. This requires honesty with yourself and others about:

How you feel.

What you're thinking.

What you've experienced.

Ephesians 4:25 says,

"Therefore each of you must put off falsehood and speak truthfully to your neighbor, for we are all members of one body."

4. What's the main point of the passage?

_____

_____

5. Colossians 3:9 reminds us that we are living as those made alive in Christ. Read the passage and write your honest thoughts about how it might apply in your life right now.

_____

_____

_____

_____

There's no need to lie. But some of us are in the habit of doing it sometimes without even realizing it. "I'm fine" is one of the most popular lies we tell! We lie to ourselves. We exaggerate. We lie by omission. Only Jesus can help us stop lying. If you struggle in this area, ask the Lord to help you and remember the truth of this passage.

CAN WE PLEASE GET OVER OURSELVES?

I remember a time in my life when I was too afraid to go into a church. I was worried that either everyone would be staring at me, or worse, that nobody would notice me. I know that sounds contradictory, but it was the truth of my insecurities at the time.

Most people you meet are not thinking about you, because they're too busy thinking about themselves.

Each of us can struggle to trust God in our moments of uncertainties and insecurities. But let me give you a truism: Most people you meet are not thinking about you, because they're too busy thinking about themselves.

6. Has there ever been a time when you opened up and shared something personal with someone and it backfired on you? Explain what happened and how it made you feel.

_____

_____

_____

7. Have you ever been in a friendship that ended because you weren't honest about your feelings early on and your hurt feelings turned into resentment? Write about it below.

_____

_____

_____

_____

_____

8. Is there a friend in your life right now that you need to talk to about something that is bothering you? Maybe your feelings are hurt and you need to express them. Maybe you need to apologize for something you said or did that is bugging you and won't go away. Use the space below to write what you want to say to that person. In a later chapter we'll talk about practical tips for how you might approach this person in your life.

_____

_____

_____

_____

_____

_____

_____

Friendship Challenge
#7

Begin praying that God would reveal any friendship in which you need to be more honest and real so that you can experience a deeper, more meaningful relationship.

DAY 3 – A GODLY FRIEND IS TRUSTWORTHY

I threw out a question on social media asking people to give me words that describe a good friend. The overwhelming winner was the word, "trustworthy."

1. In your life experience, what does it look like to be, or to have, a trustworthy friend?

    _____

    _____

    _____

    _____

Scripture is clear when it says to trust God with all your heart (Proverbs 3:5).

When we start trusting people, however, it can lead to danger because only Jesus can save us. When we put our trust in humans, we will be let down because, well, we're human. Far from perfect. Even good friends will let us down on occasion; and in the same way, we will disappoint others.

Let's face it: we all fall short of being 100% trustworthy.

It's a good thing Scripture never says to trust in man fully, or we would all be doomed. The Bible says to love others as yourself (Mark 12:31), put others before yourself (Philippians 2:3), serve one another (Galatians 5:13), but put your full trust in God (Proverbs 3:5).

God never lies, He never slanders, He never makes fun of us, He understands all our pain, He promises always to be there, and faithfulness and loyalty is part of His character.

 The only way to have a friend is to be one.

————— Ralph Waldo Emerson

FAITHFUL FRIENDS

But what about our friends? We long to trust people. We need our friends to point us to God as the true source of trust. So let's shift the language and talk about godly friends being faithful and trustworthy.

2. Read and write out Proverbs 20:6

_____

_____

A trustworthy friend offers a voice of reality to remind us where we came from.

3. Read Proverbs 11:13. What's the main point?

_____

_____

LOVE IN ACTION

We often hear 1 Corinthians 13 read when we attend weddings, but much of it applies to friendships too. A true friend is called to love at all times. Now let me be clear that this does not mean that you are to accept sin in your friend's life, but it does mean that you protect, trust, hope, and persevere with godly friends (1 Corinthians 13:7).

4. Read James 2:26. How does this verse apply to friendship and trust?

_____

_____

5. Look up Matthew 5:37 and write the main idea.

_____

_____

_____

> ❝ A friend is one who overlooks your broken fence and admires the flowers in your garden.
>
> Unknown

TRUSTWORTHY

Do your friends find you trustworthy in everyday life and in their time of need? How do you practice being faithful? Here are some other words people mentioned on social media, add your own words in the margin.

Accepting	Graceful	Secure
Available	Truth speaking	Sincere
Compassionate	Intentional	Steadfast
Discreet	Kind	Supportive
Dependable	Loving	Transparent
Faithful	Loyal	Unconditional
Forgiving	Non-competitive	Understanding
Fun	Nurturing	Unselfish
Genuine	Reliable	Vulnerable
A Good Listener	Respectful	Wise

Friendship Challenge

#8

Ask the Lord to show you if there is a friend in your life that you have not been trustworthy with in the past.

Pray for the courage to talk to this friend. And, remember, you can do hard things even if they are uncomfortable.

" By God's grace, a tested friendship grows into a stronger friendship.

DAY 4 — A GODLY FRIEND IS DISCERNING

1. Write about a time when you blurted out something to a friend that you immediately regretted. If you can't think of an example, reflect on a time when a friend unintentionally hurt your feelings.

   _____

   _____

   _____

   _____

   _____

   _____

Discernment is a delicate balance between our responsibility to know God's Word and our ability to be aware of the counsel of the Holy Spirit.

Regret. Hurt feelings. Poor counsel. These things happen when we don't practice discernment in our friendships.

It takes practice.

We need our friends to speak truth into our lives, and we need to do the same for them. That's how friendships deepen, and how we grow as followers of Jesus.

While the Bible teaches that discernment is a gift of the Spirit (1 Corinthians 12:10), it also says that we can ask God for it.

2. Look up James 1:5 and answer the following questions:
   - What are God's instructions?_____
   - What will God do if you ask? _____

3. In the following Scripture, mark the things that the Spirit of God will do in the lives of believers.
   "But when he, the Spirit of truth, comes, he will guide you into all the truth. He will not speak on his own; he will speak only what he hears, and he will tell you what is yet to come." John 16:13

PRACTICING DISCERNMENT

No friend needs a knee-jerk reaction or a biased opinion. Deep and meaningful friendships rely on the Holy Spirit's guidance and wisdom. Here are some tips for practicing discernment in your friendships so that you can speak wisdom with truth and love.

- Stay in God's Word.

- Ask Him for wisdom in your friendships.

- Pray that He will reveal His perfect timing when you need to speak truth to a friend.

- Practice observation, so you know when your friend's heart is too tender for rebuke, or she needs a kick in the pants from someone she trusts and loves.

4. What would you add to this list?

_____

_____

_____

5. Read Philippians 1:9-11, below, and mark the things that Paul is praying for you, as a believer in Christ, in these verses.

"And this is my prayer: that your love may abound more and more in knowledge and depth of insight, so that you may be able to discern what is best and may be pure and blameless for the day of Christ, filled with the fruit of righteousness that comes through Jesus Christ—to the glory and praise of God." Philippians 1:9-11

6. As you reflect on Philippians 1:9-11, how do you think these truths can make you a more discerning friend?

_____

_____

_____

_____

_____

_____

_____

_____

_____

_____

" Timely advice is lovely, like golden apples in a silver basket.

Proverbs 25:11 NLT

Friendship Challenge #9

Think about the habits that hinder or help your ability to discern God's truth and decide to work on improving that habit.

DAY 5 – A GODLY FRIEND IS INTENTIONAL

1. In what area(s) of your life are you consistent and intentional?

_____

_____

_____

_____

_____

Deep and meaningful friendships don't happen by accident. We must be intentional. Whether a casual gathering or a tough conversation, being present physically, emotionally, and spiritually is the foundation of any good relationship.

Turn off your phone and be present when you're with your friend if you want to deepen your relationship, especially if you're with someone you don't get to see often. Time is precious. Make sure that you are honoring her time with your full attention.

BE INTENTIONAL – DESPITE FEELINGS OR CIRCUMSTANCES

I can be a flaky friend. I dislike this about myself, but it's true. My intentions are good, but I get busy, or forgetful, or depressed, and simply don't follow through with what I said I was going to do. I've always let myself off the hook; but lately, God has impressed upon me the importance of being consistent and intentional. Whether I feel like it or not.

Can you relate?

We judge ourselves based on our intentions while other people judge us based on our actions.

Remember that godly friendships are not only a gift but also a blessing. When you enter into these kinds of relationships, you will grow in ways that you wouldn't otherwise. When you walk with someone else by your side who wants to become more like Christ, your faith and relationship with God will transform.

BE INTENTIONAL — ESPECIALLY WHEN THINGS GET UNCOMFORTABLE

I hate conflict! I don't want to feel uncomfortable. I would rather avoid, ignore, or pretend that things are okay than confront in love. But I have learned over the years if I want to keep becoming more like Christ, if I want to love well, then I need to be willing to have awkward conversations and acknowledge when things are off in a friendship.

2. How can the words of James 4:6 help you when you need to have a hard conversation with a friend?

_____

_____

_____

_____

_____

BE INTENTIONAL — WHEN YOU NEED TO EXPERIENCE OR GIVE GOD'S GRACE

Friends are those rare people who ask how we are and then wait to hear the answer.

Being present physically, emotionally, and spiritually is the foundation of any good relationship. Put your phone on "do not disturb" and be present when you're with your friend.

Our friends will have flaws, and they may fall short even as it relates to your friendship, but you don't look down on them because of it. You work through these issues by encouraging each other and loving each other as Christ loved us.

3. What does Romans 15:7 command us to do, and why does it matter?

_____

_____

4. How does Proverbs 17:9 apply to the topic of being intentional with friends?

_____

5. What are some ways that you can be intentional with one or two friends this week?

_____

_____

_____

Friendship Challenge
#10

As you reflect on today's study, decide on some ways that you can be intentional with one or two friends this week.

3

Jealousy continually whispers to us, "God's gifts are not good enough."

UNHEALTHY FRIENDSHIPS

Introduction

We are broken people, and this week we'll take a look at some of the more difficult topics that exists within friendships. We'll do some self-exploration and ask ourselves some hard questions about our thinking and our behavior within friendships. We'll reflect on some painful experiences we've had with friends. Why?

Because at times relationships are messy.

People are sinful.

God wants us to have healthy relationships and that takes honesty and sometimes tough decisions.

HAVE YOU EXPERIENCED TOXIC RELATIONSHIPS?

If you've experienced friendships that were unhealthy or toxic, it's okay to be guarded, but know that there are many, many people who desire to have healthy friendships. You don't need to travel this journey alone. When you are in a vulnerable place, choose people who will direct you toward God, not draw you further away. You will know these people because their spirit of grace and love will meet you where you are today.

While you are working to build healthy friendships, pursue wisdom.

God and His Word are your best sources for care and advice.

And remember the promise of Philippians 2:13,
"For it is God who works in you to will and to act on behalf of His good pleasure."

HAVE YOU DISPLAYED TOXIC PATTERNS IN YOUR FRIENDSHIPS?

If you have behaved in unhealthy or toxic ways in friendships, you're not alone. Take heart, the situation isn't hopeless. It starts with honesty and a willingness to look at our own intentions and behaviors. This week we'll look at the issue of unhealthy or toxic friendships including:

- **Day 1** – Jealousy.
- **Day 2** – Codependency.
- **Day 3** – Ghosting.
- **Day 4** – Martyrs and Saviors.
- **Day 5** – Steps Forward.

LET'S PRAY

"God grant me the serenity to accept the people I cannot change, the courage to change the one I can, and the wisdom to know it's me." Amen.

DAY 1 – JEALOUSY, A SNEAKY FRIENDSHIP KILLER

Begin your time by praying Psalm 139:23-24,

"Search me, O God, and know my heart; test me and know my concerns. See if there is any offensive way in me; lead me in the way everlasting."

Jealousy is toxic: whether we're the victim or offender, jealousy is about control and dissatisfaction.

1. Remember a time that you were jealous or envious. What ran through your mind? How did you respond?

   _____

   _____

   _____

   _____

   _____

Most of us don't like to admit that we get jealous or envious. But in reality these feelings are so common that we tend to overlook them. We minimize their sinfulness and allow them to fester to the point of damaging our soul. Let's define the difference between the two words.

- To envy is to want something which belongs to another person. "You shall not covet your neighbor's house, his wife or his servant, his ox or donkey or anything that belongs to your neighbor."(Exodus 20:17)

- To be jealous is to fear that something we possess will be taken away by another person. Jealousy can apply to our jobs, our possessions, or our reputations, but the word more often refers to anxiety which comes when we are afraid that the affections of a loved one might be lost to a rival. In friendship, we fear that our friends will be lured away by someone else who, when compared to us, seems to be more attractive, capable, or successful.

Either way, jealously and envy are part of our sinful nature. They both cause us to idolize things or people over God. For purposes of this study, we are going to use the words interchangeably. Jealousy and envy are soul-enemies, and Scripture warns us against them over and over.

2. Read Galatians 5:19-21 and answer the question below.
   - In verse 19, what does Paul call jealousy and envy?

_____

At first glance, you might wonder why jealousy would appear in a list with such dreadful sins. But envy is a condition of the heart, and being on this list reminds us that when we are jealous we are not satisfied with what God has already provided. And, we must live by the spirit not the flesh (Galatians 5:16-17).

3. Read the following passages and write down the impact of jealousy:

- Proverbs 6:34

_____

- Proverbs 14:30

_____

- Proverbs 27:4

_____

- James 3:14-16

_____

However jealousy or envy present themselves, we must actively move to resolve these internal struggles to have healthy friendships.

CORE ISSUES OF JEALOUSY

Scripture tells us that jealousy is the opposite of love (1 Corinthians 13:4), a symptom of pride (1 Timothy 6:3-5), a cause of conflict (James 3:16), and a sign of unbelievers (Romans 1:29).

But what's underneath jealously?

- **A discontented heart.** It's easy to look at other people and wish we had what they have instead of being satisfied with what God has provided us. Consider this passage in James.

  "You want what you don't have, so you scheme and kill to get it. You are jealous of what others have, but you can't get it, so you fight and wage war to take it away from them. Yet you don't have what you want because you don't ask God for it. And even when you ask, you don't get it because your motives are all wrong—you want only what will give you pleasure." James 4:2-3 NLT

- **Pride.** Why do so many of us have this ingrained attitude that we are entitled to things? We want recognition or popularity, we notice likes and followers on social media. When we are jealous, it's usually because we have our eyes on ourselves.

"For all that is in the world—the desires of the flesh and the desires of the eyes and pride in possessions—is not from the Father but is from the world." 1 John 2:16 ESV

- **Insecurity/Fear.** When we think we're not good enough or have a poor self image we're vulnerable to jealousy. Insecurity whispers, "She doesn't have time for me," or "I can't go to church alone." Fear and insecurity lead to jealousy and keep you from living the life that God wants for you.

- **Self-pity.** A prime example of self-pity is found in King Ahab's wicked life. Ahab coveted a vineyard belonging to Naboth and wanted to buy it. But when his neighbor refused to sell,

"Ahab went home, sullen and angry … He lay on his bed sulking and refused to eat." 1 Kings 21:4

Imagine, a king pouting in his palace! So full of jealously. So full of himself.

4. Which of these core issues do you relate to the most? Explain.

_____

_____

_____

_____

_____

_____

BEING ON THE RECEIVING END OF JEALOUSY

I felt sick to my stomach when I read these words in an email from a childhood friend, "You're constantly telling me how great you are, how wonderful your kids are, what a great mom you are, blah, blah, blah! You make me feel judged and criticized by you."

This was from a godly woman who I thought practiced authenticity and transparency in our relationship. Someone who had prayed with me, cried with me, shared with me, and showed up for me. For 30 years.

I had no idea she felt this way. When I shared the victories of our family, she responded with excitement. So, I naturally assumed she was sharing in my celebration.

I was wrong.

Jesus was full of grace and truth. Not one without the other.

I never picked up on her jealousy. And I never knew she felt criticized by anything I said. I certainly never intended to cause hurt. In all those years she never approached me with truth and grace as Christians are commanded to do throughout Scripture. I wonder how our relationship would have been different if we could have talked about the issue sooner.

Jesus was full of grace and truth. Not one without the other. Both. We are to imitate Jesus and this applies to our friendships as well. Live a life of truth and grace with your friends.

Friends should be building you up and celebrating your successes, but if they are jealous and choose not to confess their jealousy or get to the root of it, here are some steps you can take.

- Pray that God would reveal what needs to be changed in the relationship and if/how you may need to take action.

- Talk to your friend and ask them if they are having negative feelings about you or if you did something to offend them. Be honest that you've noticed a negative reaction and would love to clear things up if needed. Use the example of Christ.

  "For the law was given through Moses; grace and truth came through Jesus Christ." John 1:17

- Distance yourself from the unhealthy person. I know, distancing yourself from a friend is awful, but sometimes it is exactly what you need to do. We'll talk more about boundaries later this week.

Friendship Challenge #11

This week ask the Holy Spirit to heighten your awareness of jealousy and envy in your friendships. When you realize you're experiencing these feelings, confess them to the Father and ask Him what to do about it.

"**An Adult Codependent Relationship** is when you choose to be responsible *for* someone else.

An Adult Interdependent Relationship is when you are mutually responsible *to* each other."

DAY 2 — CODEPENDENCY

1. Do you struggle with a desire to control other people or tell them how to fix their problems? Explain.

   _____

   _____

   _____

   _____

   _____

2. Do you find yourself wanting to protect your friends and family from the natural consequences of their behavior? If yes, write an example. If no, write about a time you've observed this in someone else.

   _____

   _____

   _____

   _____

   _____

   _____

   _____

   _____

   _____

   _____

"Codependent" is a word that is thrown around often but can be challenging to explain. When I googled the term "codependency," in less than a second the search came back with about 8,460,000 results. YIKES!

Codependency is a part of our human brokenness and it can deeply impact friendships.

Here's a definition from the Focus on the Family website:

> "Codependency is a coping mechanism used compulsively by people trying to find personal worth and value by meeting the perceived needs of others," writes Russ Rainey, Ph.D. "The bottom line is," Rainey continues, "codependency is a mixed-up motivation to help. Helping becomes a have to out of a sense of guilt and survival instead of a want to out of a spirit of voluntary service."

Perfectionism and caretaking are both paths that leads the codependent to experience anxiety, depression, anger, resentment, and hurt.

Not all codependents grew up in an alcoholic or abusive home. Sometimes there was a physical or mental illness, emotional instability, trauma, or emotionally absent parents. Countless situations lead to codependent behavioral patterns and emotional difficulties.

Notice that it is "co" dependent. That means at least two people are involved. The person who has the desire to fix, and the person who depends on that person to rescue them from whatever situation they are in – lack of finances due to poor choices, lack of self-esteem, poor family dynamics – the list is endless. A codependent will work on the other person's problem more than the person who actually has the problem!

Breaking away from codependent friends can be challenging.

Recognizing and accepting codependent belief patterns in our own lives takes time.

We first need the Lord to help us recognize our tendencies to control and our desire to base our self-worth on the opinions and approval of other people. But with courage, humility, and hard work, you can learn to see and begin to change codependent behavior.

It's OK to lovingly distance yourself from a friend who exhibits codependent behavior.

It's alright if you see yourself in this lesson.

It's OK to lovingly distance yourself from a friend who exhibits codependent behavior.

It's alright if you see yourself in this lesson.

PROFILE OF A CODEPENDENT

At the root of codependency is the lie of shame-based thinking. As a child, my needs for love, security, worth, and significance were not met. As a result, I grew up feeling ashamed of my feelings and unable to identify my basic wants and needs.

By the time I became an adult, I was an expert at denying, devaluing, and repressing my emotions to avoid the shame I felt for merely being me. Please know that these deeply held patterns of thinking were outside of my consciousness. To cope with this, I became a perfectionist. I embraced the lie that IF I could control everything and everyone around me, I would feel secure.

Some codependents take the caretaking route choosing to put others' feelings and needs above their own. Either path leads the codependent to experience anxiety, depression, anger, resentment, and hurt because of the belief that nobody cares. Until we get help, all codependents experience a perpetual cycle of fear, shame, blame, and self-hate.

INTERNAL BOUNDARIES

Codependents lack healthy inner boundaries. These internal boundaries dictate how we share our reality. These boundaries inform us whether our words, tone, manner, intensity, intention, and content are appropriate.

- Too Rigid – When our inner boundary is too rigid, we hold things inside and don't share at all. We have a wall up and nothing can get out.

- Too Loose – When our inner boundary is too loose or nonexistent, we spew on others, giving far more than they need or want, often causing harm. TMI.

It can be hard to discern when we may be crossing the line between Christianity and codependency. The difference between serving from a healthy place and being a codependent person, is the motivation behind why you choose to help others.

How would you honestly answer the following:

- Do you do more than your share at work, at home, or in organizations?
- Do you resist asking for help? Do you think everyone's feelings are more important than your own?
- Do you avoid confrontation?
- Do you feel responsible for the actions of others?
- Do you neglect your own needs to attend to someone else first?
- Do you accept verbal or physical abuse by others?
- Do you feel shame when other people make mistakes?
- Do you need other people's validation to feel good about yourself?
- Do you suffer from low self-esteem?

If you answered "yes" to any or all of these questions, (and most of us can admit to at least one) good news! **God wants to grow you into healthier behavior. We'll get into that more later, but know that the answers are in His Word, the Holy Bible.**

CAN YOU SEE IT?

Whether you're discovering some codependent behavior in yourself or in a friend, there is hope in Christ Jesus and freedom through the cross.

3. Can you think of a time when you were told something like, "You're making me so angry" or "You're making us look bad"? Write about the experience and how it made you feel.

_____

_____

_____

_____

_____

_____

If you hear statements like this repeatedly, it can send a message to your unconscious self that your behavior, or even your very existence, can control the feelings, actions, or opinions of other people. If these kinds of statements are repeated often enough (in childhood or adulthood) you might accept it as fact.

This is simply not true.

You can not control what other people feel or do. You are in charge of your feelings and your actions. Period.

I love the way the New Living Translation renders this Colossians passage about control, check it out,

> *"For through him [Jesus] God created everything in the heavenly realms and on earth. He made the things we can see and the things we can't see—such as thrones, kingdoms, rulers, and authorities in the unseen world. Everything was created through him and for him. He existed before anything else, and he holds all creation together." Colossians 1:16-17*

" You can not control how other people feel or what they do.

WHAT IF?

The Lord God most high, wants us to look to Him first to meet our needs. He desires for each of us to depend on Him. Sometimes the best thing we can do is get out of the way so God can be God – not only in our lives, but also in the lives of the people we love.

I want to ask you some rhetorical questions. You can move swiftly through this part of the lesson; OR, you can let the questions penetrate deeply into your core allowing the Holy Spirit to change you.

Please don't miss out. Ready?

- What if I believed what God says is true? I mean, really true. Like deep down in my core, nothing in all creation will ever change my mind, real!

  "As for God, His way is perfect; the word of the LORD is flawless. He is a shield to all who take refuge in Him." Psalm 18:30

- What if I looked at others less and God more?

  "Let us fix our eyes on Jesus, the author, and perfecter of our faith, who for the joy set before Him endured the cross, scorning its shame, and sat down at the right hand of the throne of God." Hebrews 12:2

- What if I let Christ be my source of love and not look to people for approval?

  "The LORD appeared to us in the past, saying: I have loved you with an everlasting love; I have drawn you with loving-kindness." Jeremiah 31:3

Sister, don't just read it; let it go deep.

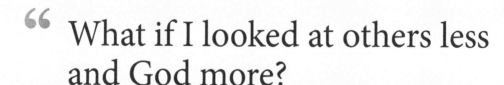

" What if I looked at others less and God more?

- What if I judged others less and let God deal with me more?

"Work at living in peace with everyone, and work at living a holy life, for those who are not holy will not see the Lord. Look after each other so that none of you fails to receive the grace of God. Watch out that no poisonous root of bitterness grows up to trouble you, corrupting many." Hebrews 12:14-15 NLT

You may want to check out Celebrate Recovery® to learn more about how to have healthy relationships.

www.CelebrateRecovery.com

- What if I believed that when I called on God, He heard my prayers, and is acting on my behalf?

"God is our refuge and strength, a very present help in trouble. Therefore we will not fear though the earth gives way, though the mountains be moved into the heart of the sea, though its waters roar and foam, though the mountains tremble at its swelling." Psalm 46:1-3

Reread it, friend, slowly and intentionally.

Friendship Challenge #12

This week, be a friend to yourself and earnestly pray Lamentations 3:40.

Talk to a trusted friend or counselor about things that may have been stirred up through this lesson. Whether you're discovering some codependent behavior in yourself or in a friend, there is hope in Christ Jesus and freedom through the cross.

DAY 3 — WHEN A FRIEND DISAPPEARS (GHOSTING)

1. Have you ever had somebody quit a relationship with you by totally cutting off all communication with no explanation? Have you ever been guilty of ghosting a friend? Describe the situation.

_____

_____

_____

_____

_____

_____

_____

When a friend disappears by ghosting you, it's because of something going on in her life, not yours. Immaturity or fear is usually at the root of such behavior.

Ghosting is when a person wholly and unexpectedly severs all communication with another person without any explanation. Blocks your phone number. Blocks social media profiles. No goodbye. No, "I'm mad." No clue it was coming. Just gone. If you were to run into them in a public place, they would likely turn around and walk the other way. Wow. Ghosting is …

Painful. Confusing. Immature.

The first thing to know is that if you have been ghosted, it's not about you. When a friend disappears in this manner, it's because of something going on in her life, not yours. Immaturity or fear is usually at the root of such behavior.

If you've been guilty of such behavior, take heart, sister, you are not alone. And, with prayer, practice, and some wise counsel, you can move toward healthy relationships whether or not that one can be repaired.

2. Read Proverbs 18:24. What stands out to you in this passage?

_____

_____

_____

_____

_____

In 1 Corinthians, we read about the type of company we keep. I love the way the Contemporary English Version renders this passage.

"Don't fool yourselves. Bad friends will destroy you." 1 Corinthians 15:33

We're all capable of wrong behaviors in friendships. Let's keep pressing into this tough topic.

3. Read Romans 7:18 while thinking about friendships. What comes to mind as you read this passage?

_____

_____

_____

_____

AVOIDING UNCOMFORTABLE CONVERSATIONS

Most of the time, when ghosting occurs it's because someone is avoiding a hard conversation. They let fear get the best of them and decide it's easier to run away than it is to address conflict, or jealousy, or other inappropriate behavior. So, they choose the easy way out. They cut you off.

Read Proverbs 27:5-6

"Better an open rebuke than love that is concealed. The wounds of a friend are faithful, but the kisses of an enemy are deceitful."

In healthy relationships, we don't avoid hard conversations. More about this next week, but for now just know if you've been ghosted it's not your fault.

> " When ghosting occurs it's usually because someone is avoiding an uncomfortable conversation.

HOW YOU CHOOSE TO RESPOND

How you chose to respond to ghosting is your choice. It's the only thing that you can control. Here are some things to consider:

- **Pray for your friend.** Ask God to have His way in that person's heart.

- **Pray for yourself.** Look up and pray Psalm 139:23-24 aloud. Ask the Lord to show you if you have any part in what happened. Even if you can't talk to this now former-friend, you can make things right between you and God and take the knowledge into future relationships.

- **Acknowledge the reality of the pain.** Don't minimize the hurt, but spend the least amount of emotional energy as possible thinking about it. Does that make sense?

4. Read 1 Peter 5:6-7.

   - What is God asking you to do?

   _____

   - What do you learn about God in these verses?

   _____

5. Remember the never-failing presence of God. Read Deuteronomy 31:6 and Isaiah 49:15.

   - What are the themes of these two verses?

   _____

   _____

6. Forgive and release them. Romans 12:18 instructs us,

   "If it is possible, as far as it depends on you, live at peace with everyone."

You have the choice to forgive your friend for their immaturity expressed through ghosting.

If you don't forgive them, you'll bring resentment and fear into the next relationship. We'll spend an entire day on the topic of forgiveness next week; but for now, reflect on today's passages and ask God to help you forgive.

Friendship Challenge #13

If you have a pattern of ghosting, then ask God to humbly help you with renewing your mind. Reflect for a moment and ask the Lord to reveal to you, by His Spirit, any action that you need to take to address unresolved issues in friendships. Perhaps it's time to seek counseling to discover what areas you may be afraid to confront within yourself.

DAY 4 — MARTYRS AND SAVIORS

1. What or whom do you think of when you see the phrase, "Drama Mama?" Note: This is an internal question not to be shared with others so that we're not gossiping.

_____

_____

_____

_____

_____

When looking at drama within the context of friendships we see it play out in a couple of common ways.

- **The Martyr Complex** refers to someone who feels the need to sacrifice herself for somebody else's sake. She might loudly and frequently make statements like these:

  "Never mind, I will do it, I always have to do it or it won't get done!"

  "There I was slaving in the kitchen and nobody would come to help me!"

- **The Savior Complex** refers to someone who feels the need to constantly save someone else. You might hear her make these types of comments:

  "What would they do without me? I swear if I weren't around they would starve to death."

  "So I TOLD them what they needed to do because clearly they couldn't figure it out without my input."

If they seem similar it's because they are two ways of looking at the same issue. People with a martyr or savior complex subconsciously or consciously seek attention by creating drama. And like so many things we are studying about in friendships, it's not the action itself that is the issue but the intention behind the behavior. Let me be clear, it is not wrong to sacrifice for someone if your motives are true, noble, right, and pure (see Philippians 4:8-9).

2. Proverbs is full of wisdom about toxic friendships. Look up these passages and jot down characteristics described in each one that can feed into drama.

- Proverbs 14:15 _____
- Proverbs 20:19 _____
- Proverbs 22:24-25 _____
- Proverbs 24:21-22 _____
- Proverbs 28:7 _____
- Proverbs 29:3 _____

3. Which of these characteristics do you see in yourself? Reflect for a moment and ask the Lord to reveal to you, by His Spirit, any propensity you have towards unhealthy relationships.

_____

_____

BEHIND THE SCREEN

Technology has shifted the definition of friendship in recent years. With the click of a button, we can add a "friend" or make a new connection. But having hundreds of online friends is not the same as having a close friend you can spend time with in person. We'll talk more about this topic in Week 4. Online friends can't hug you when a crisis hits, visit you when you're sick, or celebrate a happy occasion with you. But you know what they can do?

CREATE DRAMA!

It's so easy to hide behind a screen with inappropriate behavior. It doesn't take much guts to slander, judge, exaggerate, call people out, or generally create drama online. It's as if the world has become more vocal about their opinions with zero filters. Social media is a perfect platform for the drama llama.

THE REALITY AND THE ANTIDOTE

The real reason people struggle with a martyr or savior complex is because drama is a distraction. The issues in our lives may be boring or monotonous or they may be too stressful to handle. Thriving off drama from the rest of the world can help us forget about hard truths of our own lives. Creating and interacting with drama can feed a savior or a martyr.

Even if you struggle with some of the characteristics we looked at above or have a tendency to catastrophize things, you know as well as I do that there is only one savior, and it's not you!

Let's remind ourselves of some truths we know from the Bible.

Some people are attracted to drama from the rest of the world because it distracts from painful parts of their own lives.

4. Read Luke 19:10 and 2 Corinthians 5:17. What do these passages say about believers in Christ?

   _____

   _____

As Christians, we are called to live differently. And, we are called to grow in our relationships with Christ and with others. Before you read the following Scriptures, ask the Lord to speak to you, through His Holy Spirit, about anything that you need to see.

> *"Do not let any unwholesome talk come out of your mouths, but only what is helpful for building others up according to their needs, that it may benefit those who listen." Ephesians 4:29*

> *"Do not lie to each other, since you have taken off your old self with its practices and have put on the new self, which is being renewed in knowledge in the image of its Creator." Colossians 3:9-10*

5. What is God, through His Holy Spirit, revealing to you through the above passages?

   _____

   _____

   _____

   _____

   _____

   _____

Friendship Challenge #14

This week, when you encounter drama, whether self-imposed or observed, choose to acknowledge it for what it is, a sin.

Talk to your friends about the subject of drama and the reality that sometimes life is difficult, and overcoming challenges is a part of adulting.

DAY 5 – STEPS FORWARD

1. We've been talking about unhealthy relationships this week, and I do not doubt that one or more of these days have hit a chord with you at some level. Take a look back at each day and reflect on what area you must identify with in your friendships. Write your thoughts.

   _____

   _____

   _____

   _____

   _____

Today, we'll look at three practical areas to help when you identify unhealthy behaviors in friendships or within yourself.

- The importance of talking things out.

- The necessity of setting boundaries.

- Why seeking God above all is essential.

START TALKING

Most of us want to avoid conflict because it's uncomfortable, but pushing through a few awkward moments keeps things real and will deepen our friendships.

Godly Boundaries come from a deep understanding of who we are, and a refusal to be defined as anything less.

The way we (and our friends) respond in these situations helps us to know how authentic our relationships really are.

- Unexpressed irritation, frustration, or jealousy will lead to anger.
- Unexpressed anger will lead to resentment.
- And unexpressed resentment can lead to an explosion. Sadly, this may lead to the end of a relationship.

But it doesn't have to.

I have found one of the best ways to practice having hard conversations is to first write what I want to say. That way, I can figure out what's really bugging me and filter through some of the raw feelings before I talk to a friend about a hurtful situation. Sometimes, I choose to read the note to my friend, so I don't forget what I want to say or get flustered with emotion or reactions.

Another helpful tip is to let your friend know that you have something you want to talk about ahead of time and that it's hard for you because you might be uncomfortable. But, because you love this friend, you want to make an effort to have the conversation.

When possible, pray before and after the conversation. The goal is to speak the truth with love and grace and to express where you have struggled.

66 God set firm boundaries from the very beginning in creation, starting with physical boundaries as He separated the heavens, earth, and sea.

BOUNDARIES DEFINED

2. When you read the word "boundaries" in a Bible study, what is your immediate reaction? Be honest.

_____

_____

_____

Merriam-Webster defines a boundary as: "Something that indicates or fixes a limit or extent."

The Oxford English Dictionary says it this way: "A line which marks the limits of an area; a dividing line."

I appreciate both of these definitions, because when we set personal boundaries we're 'drawing a line' or 'fixing a limit.' We're communicating where the actions of another person will reach the point of what is 'not OK' with us and where a healthy boundary begins.

We set boundaries to offer those we care about a choice, not to control other people.

OUR GOD IS A GOD OF BOUNDARIES

God set firm boundaries from the very beginning in creation, starting with physical boundaries as He separated the heavens, earth, and sea (Genesis 1). Then God set relational boundaries when He gave Adam his limits. He told him what he could do, what he couldn't do, and what the consequences would be if he disobeyed (Genesis 2:15-17).

All the way from Genesis to Revelation (Revelation 22:11-15) God has established His borders and plainly defined who will be allowed inside of them, and who will not.

Yes, God allows us the freedom to choose which side of the line we want to live on, but there is no denying that our God is, without question, a God of boundaries!

"Don't team up with those who are unbelievers. How can righteousness be a partner with wickedness? How can light live with darkness? What harmony can there be between Christ and the devil? How can a believer be a partner with an unbeliever? And what union can there be between God's temple and idols?" 2 Corinthians 6:14-15 NLT

Hot-tempered people must pay the penalty. If you rescue them once, you will have to do it again.

———— Proverbs 19:19 NLT

Now, use the space below to make a list on both sides of God's boundaries that appear in this passage. The first one is filled in for you, so you get the idea.

BELIEVER	UNBELIEVER
Righteous	Wicked

God's boundaries define consequences. For example, the wages of sin is death (Romans 6:23). It always has been and it always will be eternal separation from God. The only way to avoid those consequences is to operate within God's boundaries – to accept His gift of saving grace and eternal life in relationship with Him.

BOUNDARIES IN FRIENDSHIP

We set boundaries in friendship because of who we are in Christ. And because we want to follow biblical principles for living, we should never let the world define who we are or what our boundaries need to be. We set boundaries to offer those we care about a choice, not to control other people.

The hard part can be communicating our boundaries and the reasons behind them, because it's tempting to assume that other believers think as we do. Check out Appendix A, called Helpful Phrases for Healthy Boundaries, on page 130.

3. Read Proverbs 22:24-25. How does the passage apply to boundaries?

_____

_____

Take a look at Proverbs 19:19 from the New Living Translation

"Hot-tempered people must pay the penalty. If you rescue them once, you will have to do it again."

We set up boundaries to offer those we care about a choice, not to control other people.

In this passage, we learn that we are responsible TO one another but not FOR one another. When friendships are toxic, it's okay to create a boundary, either for a period of time or for good.

4. Have you had preconceptions about boundaries being a biblical concept? Has your opinion changed after doing this week's homework? If so, how?

_____

_____

_____

_____

_____

_____

_____

SEEK GOD, AND LET GO

Many Proverbs remind us that everyone cannot and should not be a close friend. Quality trumps quantity when it comes to friendship. Select your friends wisely and then stick to them.

5. Look up Proverbs 13:20.
   - What are the two types of people described?

   _____

   - What is the result of walking with fools?

   _____

6. What warnings are we given in Proverbs 22:24-25?

   _____

7. In Proverbs 12:26, what kind of person chooses friends carefully?

   _____

As painful as it can be, sometimes we need to walk away from unhealthy friendships. If you have a friend who is unwilling to grow spiritually, self-reflect, and work on healthy relationships, then it might be time to let go.

If you want to learn more about this, you can research the clinical term "detaching with love." It might not be forever, but sometimes we just need a time of separation to work on becoming more Christ-like and understand more about what an open, honest, transparent, and God-fearing friendship looks like.

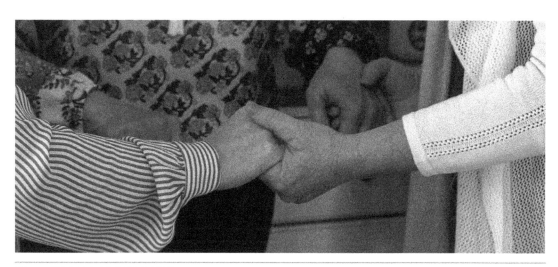

Friendship Challenge #15

Are you feeling drained, stressed, or frustrated in a friendship? If so, ask God to help you identify and give you the courage to articulate that boundary to your friend and within yourself.

See page 130 for help.

4

Friendship is a venue for great personal and spiritual growth.

WALKING IN DAY TO DAY FRIENDSHIP

Introduction

We have covered a lot of territory over these last few weeks. We've examined the "why" of friendship, the "what" of godly friendships, and the "what not" to have in a friendship.

It should be clear by now that friendship is a venue for great personal and spiritual growth. It is God-designed, and as such, He has equipped us with instructions to handle the challenges that occur within our relationships that, ultimately, give us the opportunity to fulfill our great purpose – to become more like Christ and be a light in the darkness.

Handling the bumps in a relationship requires that we "clothe" ourselves appropriately, as Colossians so beautifully instructs. Check out the amazing wardrobe we can have:

"Since God chose you to be the holy people he loves, you must clothe yourselves with tenderhearted mercy, kindness, humility, gentleness, and patience. Make allowance for each other's faults, and forgive anyone who offends you. Remember, the Lord forgave you, so you must forgive others. Above all, clothe yourselves with love, which binds us all together in perfect harmony." Colossians 3:12-14 NLT

This week we will look at how to apply this clothing to some of the issues we may face in our friendships. We'll examine:

- **Day 1** – Dealing with Trust and Betrayal.
- **Day 2** – Defining Forgiveness and Reconciliation.
- **Day 3** – Unlikely Friendships.
- **Day 4** – Social Media Friendships.
- **Day 5** – Connecting to our Ultimate Friend, Jesus Christ.

" In any relationship where trust is broken, both parties must be willing to work through the brokenness in order to heal the relationship. It is not a one sided process.

Dr. Magdalena Battles

DAY 1 – WHEN TRUST HAS BEEN BROKEN

1. Take a moment to reflect on a time when trust was broken in a friendship. What happened? How did you handle it? Did you ignore it? Address it? Are you still friends with that person?

When trust is broken, your heart changes.

_____

_____

_____

_____

_____

_____

_____

_____

We've been studying the contrast between Christ-like friends and unhealthy or toxic friends. But the reality is that they are not mutually exclusive. At times, even the best of friends (including our Christian sisters) will let us down. Just because you are a follower of Jesus doesn't make you exempt from hurting others or being hurt. See Romans 3:23.

Maybe you've had a friend break your confidence. Perhaps she gossiped about you, or blew up at you and then pretended nothing happened. Or worse, maybe she lied to you or slept with your husband.

When trust is broken, your heart changes.

Anger. Questions. Doubts. Fear. These are reasonable responses to betrayal.

Think about the life experience of Jesus. He was betrayed by Judas Iscariot into the hands of the Jewish religious leaders. One of His best friends, Peter, denied even knowing Him. And, while we know that this happened to fulfill prophecy, we also know that Jesus understood what it felt like to have trust broken.

When your heart is broken, your thoughts get broken. When this happens, sister, we have to run to the One who can put us back together.

THE GOD OF ALL COMFORT

2. Read 2 Corinthians 1:3-5.

- Why does this passage matter to followers of Christ?

  _____

  _____

- What does it mean to you that God is described as the God of ALL comfort?

  _____

  _____

Sin brings grief. We need God's comfort when we've been hurt, or when we've hurt someone else. Nowhere does He say we get to beat ourselves (or someone else) up! If you're hurting, it's OK to go to God to help you as you grieve and examine your next steps. Your feelings matter.

3. What things other than God have you turned to for comfort?

   _____

   _____

   _____

   _____

Whenever we want to run from something, we must train ourselves to run to God.

> *"For in the day of trouble he will keep me safe in his dwelling; he will hide me in the shelter of his sacred tent." Psalm 27:5*

4. Read Ephesians 2:4-5. How does this passage reflect who God is?

   _____

   _____

   _____

I'll say it again: It's OK to feel your feelings and grieve when you've experienced hurt or betrayal. But that's not the end of the journey, it's the beginning!

THE GOD OF ACTION

Let's review Colossians 3:12-14 again, written below. As you read, circle the words it uses to describe believers.

"Since God chose you to be the holy people he loves, you must clothe yourselves with tenderhearted mercy, kindness, humility, gentleness, and patience. Make allowance for each other's faults, and forgive anyone who offends you. Remember, the Lord forgave you, so you must forgive others. Above all, clothe yourselves with love, which binds us all together in perfect harmony." Colossians 3:12-14 NLT

5. List the virtues God tells us to "put on."

    _____

    _____

    _____

    _____

    _____

When you sin against your friend, what matters most is how you handle the situation.

6. Why is love the most important virtue according this passage?

    _____

    _____

    _____

One of Jesus' greatest miracles may well be that He subjected Himself to experience and feel all the things we experience and feel here on this planet. After talking to His disciples about those who would accept Him and those who would reject Him, we find these words in John 13:21:

"After saying these things, Jesus was troubled in his spirit, and testified, 'Truly, truly, I say to you, one of you will betray me.'"

"Troubled in spirit." This is Jesus we're talking about. He knew everything and had all resources available to Him along with the perfect relationship with His Father, and yet His spirit was still troubled by this betrayal. He didn't deny it – He dealt with it.

If you are faced with a betrayal in your relationships, don't allow that betrayal to blind you or embitter you. Instead, Jesus' example to us is to recognize it, grieve it, forgive it, and continue on.

Now some of you just came to a screeching halt when you read the words, "forgive it." Fear not, we'll get into what forgiveness really is later on, and it's a critical piece – try to remain open!

Handle betrayal maturely and grow from it rather than being stunted by it.

So, what did Jesus do? Instead of making the situation worse or using it as an excuse to act out, Jesus decided to come face-to-face with the issue and address it.

Don't allow betrayal to fester because it will only act as a domino effect for everything else you have going on in your life.

Handle betrayal maturely and grow from it rather than being stunted by it.

HOW TO RESPOND TO BETRAYAL

Sanctification is a translation of the Greek word, "hagiasmos," meaning "holiness" or "set apart." It's about the ongoing practical growing up in Christ. As followers of Jesus, we are not allowed to remain the same. We must keep maturing to become more like Him.

Sanctification is the same as growing in the Lord or spiritual maturity. It is a critical part of responding to betrayal.

7. Read 2 Peter 3:18 and write what followers of Christ are called to do.

_____

_____

_____

_____

We're called to respond to betrayal with truth and grace. Which is hard, because betrayal represents a loss.

Don't be surprised if you go through stages of grief. Tears can release some of the pain, and feelings of anger are natural.

The biblical model starts with a one-on-one conversation, but sometimes conversations need to happen with a third party present (see Matthew 18:15-17). One thing is for certain, rebuilding trust takes time and intentionality. And, the closer you are to the person who broke trust, the longer it will likely take to recover from what happened.

Please note: This shouldn't happen in a vacuum. If you're not sure how to approach a breach of trust, getting wise counsel is, well, wise! I'm not talking about getting your posse together in a gossip-fest; remember the goal – becoming more like Christ. With prayer, biblical counsel, wisdom, and those tools we highlighted from Colossians, we can take steps forward – even if they're baby steps.

Whether or not the relationship continues depends on the depth of the broken trust and the way that each party approaches the violation within the friendship.

We'll talk more about this tomorrow. For now, know that I am praying for you.

The closer you are to the person who broke trust, the longer it will take to recover from what happened.

Friendship Challenge #16

Is there someone you've been thinking about today as you've done this study?

Do you need to reach out to say, "I'm sorry"?

DAY 2 — FORGIVENESS AND RECONCILIATION

1. When you think of forgiveness, what's the first thing that comes to mind? Jot down your thoughts and feelings. Pay attention to your body and note any reaction you might have in your gut or any tense muscles in your jaw, shoulders, hands, or other places in your body.

_____

_____

_____

_____

_____

_____

Of all the topics we've talked about, forgiveness can be the most challenging. When someone hurts us, our natural reaction is to hurt back. Our life experiences and popular culture can convince us that bitterness and revenge is our right. And while I can absolutely relate to the desire to hold on to hurt and anger, I must learn to forgive. So must you.

2. According to the following passages, why should we forgive?

- Colossians 1:13-14

_____

_____

_____

- Ephesians 4:31-32

_____

- Matthew 6:14-15

_____

_____

When we forgive, we not only demonstrate God's love, we demonstrate love for others.

THE POWER OF FORGIVENESS

"Dear friends, since God so loved us, we also ought to love one another."
1 John 4:11

I don't know about you, but I have wasted a lot of emotional energy and space in my head by being angry and unforgiving. For many years it was a habit, and I lacked the tools and understanding to approach forgiveness from a biblical perspective.

God commands us to forgive others, just as He has forgiven us! So, it's our responsibility as Christians to love others as Christ loves us and offer forgiveness to those who offend.

Forgiveness is a GOOD thing!

Part of what was difficult for me when I was new in my Christian walk was understanding what forgiveness is NOT. So, let's spend a few minutes talking about what forgiveness is not!

FORGIVENESS IS NOT FORGETTING THE OFFENSE.

Forgive and forget – a lofty goal. For anyone who has been seriously wounded, I'm sure you'll agree with me when I say, "I wish it were that easy." Many dysfunctions and addictions develop out of a desire to "forget" rather than to deal with a deep hurt.

> **Forgiveness does not equate to avoiding, denying, or minimizing. It does NOT mean what happened to you was OK.**

And guess what? "Forgive and forget" is not a biblical quote! According to my very brief internet search, the phrase dates back to the 1300s and became a proverb (small "p") by the mid-1500s. What the Bible DOES teach, however, is to forgive and hold no resentment. No scorecard. No wall of bitterness (Hebrews 12:15).

One Christian speaker had this to say about forgive and forget: "The challenge is not to forgive and forget, the real honor comes in one's ability to forgive and yet remember."

FORGIVENESS IS NOT AVOIDING, MINIMIZING, OR DENYING.

God is a God of truth. Our goal in our Christian walk is to learn how to live in reality – both the good and the bad.

Denying or minimizing what happened or the pain associated with it does not make it go away. You must work through it.

Many of us have people in our lives and our families that will work their entire lives to avoid, minimize, and deny. It doesn't make anything go away. Rather, it's like those horror movies where the monster is buried. Looks dead. It's out of sight. But you know what's coming, right? And it's even worse when this "dead thing" comes crawling back out of the dirt! So it is with our hurts. If you just bury them, they will forever come back to haunt you, and in ways you may not expect. But if you face the "monster" and let God help you truly deal with it, you gain freedom. And that "thing," whatever it is, will lose a tremendous amount of power.

Remember, a loving God told us to forgive. It's in our best interest to do so! Forgiveness does not equate to avoiding, denying, or minimizing. It does NOT mean what happened to you was OK.

FORGIVENESS IS NOT RECONCILIATION.

Read that again.

Surprised? Want to argue with me about this?

For years I confused forgiveness with reconciliation. I thought if I forgave, I had to pretend as if the offense never happened and continue in relationship with the person who hurt me. Perhaps this is reasonable if the offense is rare or small. But in a situation such as a toxic relationship that we discussed earlier, it can be a dangerous and even a deadly misunderstanding.

I want you to get this:
- Forgiveness takes one person - it's about freedom.

- Reconciliation takes two people - it's about relationship.

Yes, it is possible to forgive someone and still keep a healthy boundary with that person.

Now that we've covered what forgiveness is not, let's talk about what forgiveness is and how we can trust God in this area of our friendships.

FORGIVENESS IS A DECISION AND A PROCESS.

Have you ever met someone who has been through a very difficult time and they say, "Oh, it's OK, I've forgiven them, it's in the past, I'm fine."? Meanwhile their body language and tone of voice are screaming something completely different? You hear their words, but you know the truth.

> " Forgiveness takes one person *it's about freedom*
>
> Reconciliation takes two people *it's about relationship*

Some offenses are quick and relatively easy to forgive – a glass of spilled milk, so to speak. Other offenses do significant damage. In these cases, rarely is forgiveness a "once and done" event. Now, God certainly has the power to do that, but in my experience, He usually chooses to take us through a process rather than the miraculous.

Forgiveness can mean choosing, then re-choosing to forgive when the memory of the offense rears its ugly head again. That's OK. It doesn't mean you failed at forgiveness, just keep choosing well!

God's forgiveness toward us forms the foundation of our ability to extend forgiveness to others.

FORGIVENESS IS RELEASING IT TO GOD.

Check out Colossians 3:13b from the New Living Translation

"Remember, the Lord forgave you so you must forgive others."

3. Read this passage and write the four things we are commanded to do.

"But I say to you who hear, love your enemies, do good to those who hate you, bless those who curse you, pray for those who abuse you." Luke 6:27-28 ESV

_____

_____

_____

FORGIVENESS IS A GIFT TO ALL BELIEVERS.

4. Read 1 Peter 3:18 and write it in your own words.

_____

_____

_____

_____

God's forgiveness toward us forms the foundation of our ability to extend forgiveness to others. The more we understand how much we have been forgiven, the fewer excuses we have to refuse forgiveness to those who have done us harm.

"But God demonstrates his own love for us in this: While we were still sinners, Christ died for us." Romans 5:8

5. Take a few moments to think through how God has forgiven you. Write a quick prayer of thanksgiving as you remember how much you are loved.

_____

_____

_____

_____

_____

_____

Unforgiveness can be compared to a tug-of-war. Remember that game? We may be grown up now, but somehow we still manage to play this childhood pastime – only the stakes are higher. On one end, there you are. On the other is your offender. You don't want to let them "off the hook" because you want them to suffer somehow for what they did. They don't deserve your forgiveness. And so you refuse to let go. The result is that you continue to struggle with your offender and drag them along with you everywhere you go until you do one thing: drop your end of the rope.

Read Romans 12:17-18

"Do not repay anyone evil for evil. Be careful to do what is right in the eyes of everybody. If it is possible, as far as it depends on you, live at peace with everyone."

6. Live at peace with everyone … when you read this passage, does anyone come to mind? Ask the Lord to show you if there's anything you need to do that depends on you. Then, write a prayer for courage to do the right thing.

_____

_____

_____

_____

Forgiveness is not often an easy thing. It may even pain you to do so. But remember, our God is a God of comfort. He will help you do what is right.

"After you have borne these sufferings a very little while, the God of all grace, who has called you to share his eternal splendor through Christ, will himself make you whole and secure and strong."
1 Peter 5:10 Phillips

Friendship Challenge #17

Today, ask God to show you who you need to talk to about forgiveness. Then pray for courage and do the right thing even though it may be difficult.

DAY 3 — UNLIKELY FRIENDS

One of the many blessings of being a follower of Christ is that He brings people into our lives that we probably never would have invited on our own!

1. When you think about your friends and acquaintances, would you consider all these people to be similar to you? Write about an unlikely or surprising friendship in your life or one you've observed in others.

   _____

   _____

   _____

   _____

   _____

   _____

   _____

   _____

   _____

EXPANDING YOUR CIRCLES

We tend to get lumped into certain "groups" as we go through life. Have you noticed? Sometimes it's intentional. For example, churches often have "life groups" and classify them as separate groups for young married folks, or singles, or empty nesters, etc.

> " If we ignore people who are not our age, race, income bracket, or life stage that we are in, we miss out on the beauty of diversity that God has created.

Other times we simply move toward what we know without realizing it.

There is benefit in doing this to some degree – we learn from our peers. But if we push everyone out of our life who is not in the same income bracket or lifestyle that we are in, we miss out on the beauty of diversity that God has created. We miss out on what God wants for us in our own spiritual growth. Community and diversity are great together.

I love this quote from Larry Burkett, he uses it in reference to marriage, but the same is true in friendships: "If two people just alike get married, one of you is unnecessary."

We learn and grow as we connect with those who have different experiences and are in various life stages.

TIA, RAQUEL

When my husband, Kal, and I were newly married in the early nineties, we met Raquel - a single mom. She arrived in Central California on a Greyhound bus with an infant in her arms and no place to live. My husband has always had a huge heart for those in need. At the time, I was narrow-minded and lived in the world of Corporate America, convinced I was better than most people. So you can imagine how I reacted a few months later when Kal asked about Raquel moving into our renovated garage.

I felt unsure. Uncomfortable. Superior. UGH!

As our unlikely friendship grew, I was stretched in my faith and personality. We came from two different cultures, and I didn't understand a lot of our interactions. Her playful spirit and attempts to get me to "loosen up" infuriated me.

"Friendship is born at the moment when one man says to another, "What! You too? I thought that no one but myself . . ."
C.S. Lewis

But Raquel was, and is, a lover of people and a lover of Jesus. Her faith is enormous. No matter what hard times come her way, she continues to declare, "God is with me. I am still blessed."

As time went on, our friendship became deep, fun, and meaningful. We became family. Lived together. Helped raise each other's kids (hence the title, Tia). When things got tough, we would pray with each other. She in Spanish and I in English. God connected us through His Spirit, and our friendship grew. We've been through births, weddings, hospital stays, and funerals. I know that I can always count on Raquel.

Imagine all I would have missed out on if I had just "ruled her out" because of our initial differences?

BIBLICAL EXAMPLES

The Bible is full of examples of unlikely friendships: Naomi and Ruth (Ruth Chapters 1-4), Elijah and Elisha (1 and 2 Kings), and probably the most well-known friendship between David and Jonathan (1 Samuel 18). Their love and commitment to their friendship seemed unlikely because of the vast differences.

Take a look at some of the differences in their lives.

DAVID	JONATHAN
Shepherd & Musician	Prince
From the tribe of Judah	From the tribe of Benjamin
Youngest in the family	Oldest in the family
Grew up in a small town and trained as a shepherd	Grew up in a palace and trained as a warrior
Had a harp and a sling	Had his own armor
Was anointed king over Jonathan	Was in line to become king

2. Read 1 Samuel 18:1-4. What does it say about their friendship?

_____

_____

_____

_____

_____

In 1 Samuel, we read what could play out like a daytime drama. Hatred. Jealousy. Trickery. And true friendship. Jonathan discovers that his father, the King, truly wants David dead, and when he tells him he must flee, they weep together in sadness.

Read their goodbye in 1 Samuel 20:41-42.

3. Imagine what it would it be like if you treated your friends with the loyalty and love that Jonathan treated David. Record your thoughts here.

_____

_____

_____

_____

_____

_____

_____

Their commonality was in their faith in the Living God. That was the center of this unlikely friendship.

CHRIST AND MANKIND

Perhaps the greatest example of an unlikely friendship is Christ and mankind.

4. Read Philippians 2:2-8. As you do, think about a friend that imitates
    Christ in your life. Write some specific things you're thinking about.

    _____

    _____

    _____

    _____

The one who is the great I AM, walked among us. While He had the right to call us servants, He chose to call us friends (John 15:15).

"Beloved, if God so loved us, we also ought to love one another. No one has ever seen God; if we love one another, God abides in us and his love is perfected in us." 1 John 4:11-12 ESV

Once again, God sets the example. He wanted friendship with US. He placed value on US as those created in His very own image. Who are we to exclude someone simply because of differences?

Because we could look beyond our differences and focus on our love of Jesus, Raquel and I remain like sisters. Nothing blesses my heart more than when I hear Raquel call me, "My Nan."

If I hadn't allowed God to build this friendship, I would have missed out on countless blessings.

YOUR UNBELIEVING FRIENDS

We've talked about unlikely friendships, but let's get more specific. While we most definitely need friendships within our spiritual family, we must resist the urge to be cliquey or exclusive in our friendships.

How many friends do you have that do not share your faith? Is it hard for you to form relationships with those you know are unbelievers or even hostile to Christ?

Keep in mind that we are called to evangelize the lost, not be intimate with them (John 15:19, Romans 12:2, Ephesians 4:20-24).

There is nothing wrong with building a quality friendship with an unbeliever. Still, the primary focus should be to win them to Christ by sharing the gospel and demonstrating it in your life.

Remember, our friendships are not just to enhance our own lives but also to grow and be stretched and be a blessing to others. At a time when our world seems increasingly divided, God still calls us to Love. One. Another.

5. Read Matthew 5:14-16. In what practical ways can you reach out to your unbelieving friends to demonstrate genuine love for them?

_____

_____

_____

If you are a follower of Christ, God has given you the great gift and opportunity to share His light and hope with others. A great way to shine this light is to demonstrate true friendship to your unbelieving friends. Being the kind of friend we have been learning about will do more good than any sermon.

THINK ABOUT YOUR FRIENDS

Let's take a few minutes to think about our friends. I want you to make a list of your friends by answering questions below.

- Who are the friends you go to dinner with?
- Who do you call when you're in a crisis?
- Who would you take on a social weekend away?
- If you needed a ride, which friend would you ask?
- Who knows your secrets?
- Add any other friends that come to mind that aren't on this list.

_____

_____

_____

_____

Let's look again at what Scripture has to say about friendships. We've seen some of these passages before, but I want you to consider each friend on your list after you read the passages.

- *"Therefore encourage one another and build each other up, just as in fact you are doing." 1 Thessalonians 5:11*

- Proverbs 12:26

- *"People who promise things they never give are like clouds and wind that bring no rain." Proverbs 25:14 GNT*

- Proverbs 13:20

- *"Be devoted to one another in love. Honor one another above yourselves." Romans 12:10*

Great, now I want you to think about each woman on your list while you consider the following questions:

- How do you feel after you spend time together?
- Does your friend make you a better person?
- Is it a mutual friendship, where both of you give to each other?
- Can you truly be yourself while you're together?
- Do you worry about what she thinks of you?

Be willing to form your own unlikely friendships. Whether you worship in a different denomination, or there's an age gap, or your race, income, political views, or vocation is different, don't be afraid to trust God with your friendships.

Friendship Challenge #18

What "new" person can you befriend this week? Someone who just moved next door? A widow who sits by herself in church? A loner at work?

DAY 4 — THE PERILS OF SOCIAL MEDIA "FRIENDSHIPS"

OUR SELFIE-CENTERED WORLD

I want to begin this day with a prayer. Will you join me?

Father, thank you for your love and faithfulness in our lives. Thank you for technology and social media and the power you've given us to use it for good. Lord, I ask that your Holy Spirit would use the questions and the Scriptures in today's lesson to convict people deep in their hearts and minds. You know the struggles each woman has in this area of her life. So, together we ask that you convict us. Change us. Empower us by your Spirit. In Jesus' name, Amen.

1. Do you ever feel depressed after spending time on social media? If so, why do you think that is?

    _____

    _____

    _____

    _____

THE CHAOS OF COMPARISON

The competition on social media. Have you experienced it? Vacation photos, work accolades, birthday surprises, children's achievements ... it can make you feel like everything is missing and something is wrong with you. Spend a little time in its never-ending stream of everybody's highlights, and before

> " If you're using social media as a substitute for real connection, your feelings of loneliness and inadequacy will increase.

you know it, you can be spiraling into depression thinking that "they" have everything, and you have nothing. That you'll never measure up, or that you have nothing to offer. Not even a picture of a delicious meal, because all you had for dinner was a bowl of cereal.

Can you relate?

What if every like, heart, share, DM and reply we give to someone on the internet is actually taking away from our energy for offline friendships?

When jealousy or depression flares up, we know it's time to get off social media and refocus our attention on God's truth. He is our provider, we belong to Him, and contentment comes from Him alone.

2. What are some of the things you feel you truly "need" to be content? Take a moment to think about this, and don't just write the churchy answer because you're doing a Bible study.

    _____
    _____
    _____
    _____

Now, read the following passages then answer the question on the following page.

- 1 Timothy 6:6

- Hebrews 13:5

3. Look back at how you answered Question 2. How do your answers line up with these verses?

_____

_____

If you are comparing yourself to others on social media, you will never be content. In fact, you may find yourself believing lies.

HOW DO YOU KNOW YOU ARE WORTHY?

If you are not on social media to encourage or be encouraged, GET OFF!

Get 50 "likes," and we feel loved. Get "zero," and we feel rejected. Social media is not where we need to be looking for love and acceptance. Now, hear me, I'm not saying that all social media is evil. I enjoy seeing what friends and acquaintances are up to when I'm busy and can't connect in person. What I'm saying is when we post something and then wait to see who responds, it's time to check ourselves.

4. How is social media impacting the way you think about yourself or how you think about life?

_____

_____

_____

_____

_____

Some of us think more highly of ourselves than we should (Romans 12:3). Some of us easily slip into the habit of putting ourselves down, which breaks our spirit (Proverbs 17:22).

Both are wrong.

Social media can be fun, but don't make it your main source of connection. It's not an accurate representation of real life anyway. You know that.

Whether lofty or lowly, believing lies about ourselves can inhibit us from having close and genuine friendships.

We need to turn down the volume on lies and turn up the volume on God's truth.

We can re-focus and fix our eyes on Christ. Remember, He is faithful. He is true. You are who He says you are.

Look at the price that Jesus paid. He gave His life for you, that's how valuable you are to Him. You are loved because of Jesus. Not because of anything you have done. Not because of your virtue or opinions or successes. But because of Christ.

2 Corinthians 5:21 reads,

"God made him who had no sin to be sin for us, so that in him we might become the righteousness of God."

5. What do you think it means to be the righteousness of God?

_____

_____

_____

_____

In this passage, Paul uses the Greek word "dikaiosynē" to denote ethical righteousness — the kind of behavior that pleases God. But the passage is much richer. Some scholars have maintained that God's righteousness refers to his transforming righteousness. Friends, we need God's transforming power in our lives.

IS TECHNOLOGY RUINING FRIENDSHIPS?

Now, more than ever, we are connected electronically to people. I'm a big fan of the benefits of communicating through texting, emailing, and social media. But I can't help but wonder if every beep, ding, or alert from our phones is causing us to confuse being connected with being close. Sometimes, I feel like we've totally lost track of the importance of time spent together. And by "together," I mean having a conversation with each other, not being in the same room on your device with another person present. Ouch! That stung for some of you.

In 2018, The Journal of Social and Personal Relationships conducted research to determine how many hours it takes to make a friend. They established that "friendship status" was examined as a function of hours together, shared activities, and everyday talk. What they discovered is alarming in light of how little time we spend in real life with people.

Their research found that a person needs to spend 50 hours with someone to create a "casual" friendship, 90 hours with someone to become "real" friends, and 200 hours to become "close" friends.

That's a significant investment.

Real friends take time to develop.

And sister, your friends on social media are not the same as the deep and reliable friendships we've been talking about.

SO, WHAT'S THE ANSWER TO LIVING IN THIS SOCIAL MEDIA WORLD?

Use social media for good.

Show a little love.

Be encouraging.

Share beauty.

Do not use it in place of real connections with friends in real life.

> " It takes
> 50 hours to create a "casual" friendship
> 90 hours to become "real" friends
> 200 hours to become "close" friends
>
> ———— *The Journal of Social and Personal Relationships*

Friendship Challenge
#19

Spend at least two hours
face-to-face with friends instead
of on social media this week.

66 A life-changing eternal
relationship with God is not
only possible but also God's
desire for you.

DAY 5 — THE ULTIMATE FRIENDSHIP

We have covered a lot of ground these past few weeks. We've seen God's design and purpose for healthy friendships and the tools we have available to foster these friendships in our lives.

We've looked at this passage before, but it's so good that I want you to look at it again. In John 15:15, Jesus says,

> *"I no longer call you servants, because a servant does not know his master's business. Instead, I have called you friends, for everything that I learned from my Father I have made known to you."*

You are not alone if you've ever thought of God as generally loving the world but not specifically loving you.

Many of us doing this Bible study have experienced this great friendship with Christ. This unlikeliest of all unlikely friendships! What a relief to know He will never leave us or forsake us (Hebrews 13:5).

That's crazy!

But it's true!

Others of us, however, may be new to this idea of a friendship with God. Perhaps God has always felt distant to you — or even non-existent. You've thought of God as being out to get you, or just generally loving the world but not specifically loving you.

Or maybe because God is Holy, you've focused on your shortcomings rather than a God who gave everything just so He could have a relationship with you. A personal relationship. The ultimate best friend.

Since we are wanting to look truthfully at life in this study, the most essential truth is this:

You are dearly loved.

A life-changing eternal relationship with God is not only possible but also God's desire for you.

1. Read 2 Peter 3:9

    ● Is this truth hard for you to accept? Why or why not?

    _____
    _____
    _____

He does not want anyone to perish, be destroyed, or be eternally separated from Him. Wow!

DEATH'S DOOR

As I sat with a friend who was on her death bed, I asked her if she was afraid of dying. She replied, "A little. It could go either way."

Not surprised by her answer, I pressed further, asking if she would like to know for sure that she was going to Heaven. She was visibly uncomfortable, and her words were barely audible, "I messed up so bad, I just don't know."

You see, this woman had made many mistakes within her relationships. She had many regrets. But honestly, she was no different than you or me.

She had heard the truth of the gospel for decades. She attended a Christian college and even had children who are missionaries, but she had never fully surrendered to Christ. My friend missed out on the abundant life that God wanted for her on earth. Now, as she lay at death's door, I prayed she would open her heart wide to the only friend who can promise eternal life.

Jesus.

WHAT ABOUT YOU?

Do your past mistakes keep you from surrendering to Jesus?

Take a moment to think about the worst things you've ever done. Your biggest secrets. Yes, those ones. Don't worry, I'm not going to ask you to write them down or share them with anyone. I just want you to be brutally honest with yourself.

2. Now, read Hebrews 4:13.

Has it ever occurred to you that God already knows the details of your sin? It may seem obvious, but sometimes we miss this truth.

3. Look up Daniel 9:9, then write it in your own words.

_____

_____

_____

_____

Do your past mistakes keep you from surrendering to Jesus?

We all mess up sometimes. We all try to run our own lives on occasion. But, sister, there is nothing you can do to earn God's love. There is nothing that you have done that can take God's love away from you.

EARN A PLACE IN HEAVEN?

New research shows that, unlike past generations, more Christians believe they can earn their way into Heaven.

The Cultural Research Center at Arizona Christian University recently conducted a survey entitled the "American Worldview Inventory 2020." In this survey, 48% of Christians believed that if a person is generally good or does enough good things during their life, they will "earn" a place in Heaven.

I struggled with this false concept during my early years as a Christian. I had been raised in a church that taught that if I sinned, I was going to Hell. Naturally, I brought this thinking into my adult life and tried really hard to be perfect as a Christian. Thank God, this is not the truth of the Bible and I got over my perfectionism!

4. Look up Ephesians 2:8-9. According to this passage, why can't you earn your way to Heaven?

_____

_____

That's right, you can't earn eternal life. It's a gift.

Now let's take a look at Titus 3:4-7 in the New Living Bible.

"When God our Savior revealed his kindness and love, he saved us, not because of the righteous things we had done, but because of his mercy. He washed away our sins, giving us a new birth and new life through the Holy Spirit. He generously poured out the Spirit upon us through Jesus Christ our Savior. Because of his grace he made us right in his sight and gave us confidence that we will inherit eternal life."

Did you catch that? It's God's grace, not the things we do.

IT'S ABOUT JESUS

Jesus' whole purpose was to make us right with God. He demonstrates all those great characteristics of friendship we've studied these last four weeks and then did the ultimate.

He endured torture. Humiliation. Even separation from God His Father so that we wouldn't have to.

5. Read Mark 15:31-34

Jesus experienced death on the cross so that you and I could have eternal life. His death paid the price of our sins. Jesus' resurrection proves that God accepted Jesus' death as the payment for our sins. And then He did the unthinkable. He defeated death.

In Romans 4:25, we read,

"He was handed over to die because of our sins, and he was raised to life to make us right with God." NLT

Because of Jesus' death on our behalf, all we have to do is believe in Him, trusting His death as the payment for our sins – and we will be saved (Romans 10:13).

God is more concerned about your heart than the words you use in prayer.

SALVATION IS YOURS FOR THE ASKING

And so, I ask you, have you received God's gift of Jesus?

Friend, if you have never accepted Christ as your personal Lord and Savior, then I invite you to do so now. Here's a prayer to help; but honestly, God is more concerned about your heart than the words you use.

Father, I know that I've blown it so many times before and that I need help. I also know that I can do nothing to earn my way to Heaven and that Jesus Christ is the only way. I believe that Jesus came to earth, died for my sins, and then rose from the dead so that I can live with you forever. Thank you for the free gift of salvation. I ask you to come into the very core of my being and take charge of my life. I say yes to you, to your will, to your way for my life. Teach me more about your Holy Spirit and give me the desire to know you more. Amen.

" For whoever will call upon the name of the Lord will be saved.

——— Romans 10:13

6. Read Romans 10:9-10.

If you prayed that prayer for the first time in your life, please share it with your group. They will be blessed to hear your news. And, if for some reason you're feeling a little shy about sharing, that's just the enemy of God trying to keep you from confirming your salvation.

You can do it. Go ahead.

I'm rejoicing with the angels of Heaven and with you. (Luke 15:10).

BUILDING FRIENDSHIP WITH JESUS

Whether you are a brand new Christian or have been a believer for decades, you need to foster your relationship. Here are some tips for getting to know your Savior.

- Study your Bible.
- Be in community (go to church and join a small group).
- Memorize Scripture.
- Talk to Jesus through prayer and music.
- Seek out godly friendships.
- Practice the principles you've learned in this study.

Like any relationship, the more time you put into it, the deeper and more meaningful it will become. And Christ will meet all your needs when your earthly friends blow it!

SIGNING OFF, FOR NOW

Girlfriend, I'm so glad that we've spent these last weeks together. It is my prayer that as a result of studying God's Word and practicing the things you've learned, you'll experience the abundant life of significant friendship that God desires for you. Drop me a note at Nancy@StopAndBeStill.org to let me know how God has worked in your life through this study. I'd love to hear from you, with much love and appreciation.
Nancy

Friendship Challenge #20

Choose something from the bullet points to the left that you can focus on this week.

APPENDIX A

HELPFUL PHRASES FOR HEALTHY BOUNDARIES

The ability to express your needs to your friends allows your relationships to remain authentic, honest, and healthy. But sometimes we just don't know what to say or how to say it.

You can establish a boundary with kindness in your voice even if your heart is anxious about doing it. I promise, it gets easier with practice. Here are some friendship boundaries to consider and some practical language for setting boundaries in friendship.

- **How much you tell your friend** – Just because someone asks you a question doesn't mean you need to answer. Here's an example of what to say, *"I'm not comfortable sharing that right now."*

- **How reciprocal your friendship will be** – You know the friend that only calls when they need something? You can say, *"Look, I care about you, and I enjoy 'x' about you, but I have to be honest, it seems like the only time I hear from you is when you need or want something from me. This makes me feel like our friendship is one-sided. So, even though this is hard to say, I need you to know that if you want to remain friends, then I need you to express some interest in me."*

  Also, we teach people how to treat us. If you are always doing what this type of friend asks for, and find you're building a resentment about it, it might be time to simply say "no" to their requests. You'll likely find this will cut down on the number of times they contact you, if indeed they see you as more of a resource than a friend.

- **How you treat each other's time** – Some friends are clueless or disrespectful with time. They show up late, and they stay too long. It might be outside of their awareness; but if it bugs you, then it's your responsibility to say something. Here is some sample language for drawing a boundary in this area of friendship. *"I have an hour and a half to spend with you, so I'm going to set the timer because I know how easy it is to get caught up in conversation."*

  When someone is at your house, and you're ready for them to leave, you have permission to ask them to go. Yes, it might feel awkward, but we're practicing healthy relationships. Try saying something like this, *"I have enjoyed our time together, and it feels a little weird saying this, but it's time for you to go so I can "X."*

- **Saying "no" to a friend** – It's easier than you think. You don't need to offer an explanation. You just need to be direct and polite. Friends need to be able to say 'no' to each other and respect the other's boundary. If this makes you insecure or feel like you're a lousy friend for setting a limit, remember your insecurity or past experiences might be making you hesitate to say no. Here's some sample language: *"Friend, I'm sorry I won't be able to help you tomorrow."* Another example would be, *"I know you would like me to be at the event but I will be unable to attend."* If your friend presses you for a reason why, assure them that you care for them and then 1) just repeat what you said before 2) tell them you're practicing saying no.

If there's any emotional manipulation such as guilt, the silent treatment, or passive-aggressive behavior, then you need to see this as a huge red flag and make decisions accordingly.

APPENDIX B

FRIENDSHIP CHALLENGES

1. **Friendship Challenge #1**
   Close your time by praying and asking God to...
   - Open your heart to the idea of deep friendships and living in community.

   - Bless your current friends.

   - Reveal where you need to step out in faith to be a better friend.

2. **Friendship Challenge #2**
   Take action from Hebrews 10:24-25 by reaching out to a friend and asking her to meet.

3. **Friendship Challenge #3**
   Pick 2 or 3 passages from the "One Another Section" on page 18 and put them into practice this week!

4. **Friendship Challenge #4**
   Is there anything you need to change when having fun with your friends to better honor God?

5. **Friendship Challenge #5**
   Ask the Lord to reveal to you someone in your life that is hurting and how you could lovingly respond.

6. **Friendship Challenge #6**
   Look for ways to show humility in your friendships this week.

7. **Friendship Challenge #7**
   Begin praying that God would reveal any friendship in which you need to be more honest and real so that you can experience a deeper, more meaningful relationship.

8. **Friendship Challenge #8**

   Ask the Lord to show you if there is a friend in your life that you have not been trustworthy with in the past. Pray for the courage to talk to this friend. And, remember, you can do hard things even if they are uncomfortable.

9. **Friendship Challenge #9**
   Think about the habits that hinder or help your ability to discern God's truth and decide to work on improving that habit.

10. **Friendship Challenge #10**
    As you reflect on today's study, decide on some ways that you can be intentional with one or two friends this week.

11. Friendship Challenge #11

This week ask the Holy Spirit to heighten your awareness of jealousy and envy in your friendships. When you realize you're experiencing these feelings, confess them to the Father and ask Him what to do about it.

12. Friendship Challenge #12

This week, be a friend to yourself and earnestly pray Lamentations 3:40. Talk to a trusted friend or counselor about things that may have been stirred up through this lesson. Whether you're discovering some codependent behavior in yourself or in a friend, there is hope in Christ Jesus and freedom through the cross.

13. Friendship Challenge #13

If you have a pattern of ghosting, then ask God to humbly help you with renewing your mind. Reflect for a moment and ask the Lord to reveal to you, by His Spirit, any action that you need to take to address unresolved issues in friendships. Perhaps it's time to seek counseling to discover what areas you may be afraid to confront within yourself.

14. Friendship Challenge #14

This week, when you encounter drama, whether self-imposed or observed, choose to acknowledge it for what it is, a sin. Talk to your friends about the subject of drama and the reality that sometimes life is difficult, and overcoming challenges is a part of adulting.

15. Friendship Challenge #15

Are you feeling drained, stressed, or frustrated in a friendship? If so, ask God to help you identify and give you the courage to articulate that boundary to your friend and within yourself. See page 130 for help.

16. Friendship Challenge #16

Is there someone you've been thinking about today as you've done this study? Do you need to reach out to say, "I'm sorry"?

17. Friendship Challenge #17

Today, ask God to show you who you need to talk to about forgiveness. Then pray for courage and do the right thing even though it may be difficult.

18. Friendship Challenge #18

What "new" person can you befriend this week? Someone who just moved next door? A widow who sits by herself in church? A loner at work?

19. Friendship Challenge #19

Spend at least two hours face-to-face with friends instead of on social media this week.

20. Friendship Challenge #20

Choose something from the bullet points on page 126 that you can focus on this week.

THANK YOU

Special thanks to Kimberly and Paul Carlson for their fantastic photography skills and the following women of NorthPointe who so graciously participated as our "models."

1. Tasha Archuleta
2. Nancy Avera
3. Julie Brager
4. Ashton Buchnoff
5. Anna Carlson
6. Kimberly Carlson
7. Jessica Carrillo
8. Emma Ceja
9. Meaghan Cochran
10. Andrea Darlow
11. Olivia Foglio
12. Ashlie Graef
13. Claire Goosev
14. Hiroko Guido
15. Kasey Jackson
16. Kayla Jenkins
17. Sally Jennings
18. Taylor McDougall
19. Christy Manning
20. Gianna Phillips
21. Keri Swobe

CPSIA information can be obtained
at www.ICGtesting.com
Printed in the USA
JSHW072017150323
38975JS00003B/6